With good wishes from
[signature]

A SOUTHEND CHILDHOOD

The thirties and forties relived

JIM WORSDALE

First published 2001

© Jim Worsdale 2001

Published by Jim Worsdale
62 Leitrim Avenue
Shoeburyness
Essex SS3 9HF

ISBN 0 9533685 1 3

All rights reserved. No reproduction permitted without prior permisssion of publisher/author.

Printed by
MGA Printing
52 - 54 Milton Road
Westcliff-on-Sea
Essex SS0 7JX

For my family

BY THE SAME AUTHOR:

Maud & Joe: A true love story of Southend

Rambling Reporter

Southend at War

True Tales from a Son of Southend

CONTENTS

Chapter 1, Page 1: Born at Number Ten

Chapter 2, Page 8: Escape from Dracula's haunt

Chapter 3, Page 12: Having a real ball

Chapter 4, Page 19: Learning the hard way

Chapter 5, Page 28: The happy weigh ahead

Chapter 6, Page 37: Copping-it on The Mile

Chapter 7, Page 43: Marbles, flicksies and more

Chapter 8, Page 52: Staying and paying guests

Chapter 9, Page 60: Drinking-in the sights

Chapter 10, Page 67: Sadness down Memory Lane

Chapter 11, Page 78: Special smells and sawdust

Chapter 12, Page 85: The fabulous Flicks

Chapter 13, Page 97: The reign of King Cole

Chapter 14, Page 103: Sunday School and soccer lessons

Chapter 15, Page 111: Learning some grown-up games

Chapter 16, Page 118: Our pier without peer

Chapter 17, Page 126: Sausage, mash and more

Chapter 18, Page 131: Back to the future

WELL, NOW...

SINCE few copies of this journal are likely to be bought or read outside the Borough of Southend-on-Sea or its immediate surrounds, I must assume that I will be preaching to the mainly converted: addressing an audience whose majority agree with me in agreeing with the Town Council's marketing slogan that Southend-on-Sea is The Place To Be. Those who disagree might be well advised to seek different surroundings, no offence intended.

Southend is the place where I have been since my birth in April 1933, give or take the occasional foray to distant parts in pursuit of journalistic work. And though, long ago, I crossed the Atlantic for a brief, working stay and the possibility of longterm absence from my original roots, I did in the event come back home.

Some two-thirds of my fifty-odd years in the newspaper business (some of them very odd indeed) have been spent in Southend as, variously, reporter, sub-editor, page designer, manager, editor. Publications on which I have earned a richly-rewarding, if never financially spectacular, living include the Southend Standard, Southend and County Pictorial and Telegraph, Southend Star, Southend Evening Echo, Southend News, Southend Observer. I looked forward to every working day, evening or night. Now I am looking back.

I suppose I fell in love with Southend from an early age. I can but say that I have loved her for as long as I can remember and I miss her when we are parted for any length of time. Southend is bawdy and beautiful; heady and heartbreaking; young in history, yet weary and aged in parts. She can be annoyingly frustrating, provoking unfavourable comment and criticism. She can be challenging and cheering and cheap and charming.

She is so many things to so many people. She is coarse and she is cultured. She is The Sun and The Times. She is suffering from disease of her heart, badly needing remedial treatment and replacement of parts. She merits a makeover and a facelift. But behind the part-worn, part-faded exterior there is beauty and attractiveness that is difficult to define and which might be recognised only by those who truly want to see it and acknowledge it and appreciate it.

Southend is full of promise and full of disappointment. Southend is fun and frustrating. Southend is many parts bound into a whole by historic statute, so that it is both rundown and uplifting, smart and seedy, upmarket and down in the dumps.

Southend is a place of a splendid yesterday and a wonderful tomorrow that is always still to arrive. The good old days are long gone and the even better days are words of politicians or dreamers.

Southend provokes in me the need to pry and question and criticise, because I want Southend to be great. And yet I will defend Southend against the attacks and the snipes of those from outside who may see and select only what they choose, in support of their view from down their noses.

Southend is my home. I began to report on it and write about it when I became a trainee journalist as the 1940s were dying. In this book I concentrate mostly on that time when I was not a writer of anything more than the occasional letter or a composition at school: of my life and times up to that day I went to work for a living at the age of fifteen.

Boyhood was brilliant – even though it encompassed hard times, wartime and austere times. I relive it in the following pages.

1

I HAVE no claims to fame, none at all. I am a simple and simply contented son of Southend who for no particular reason other than to find a peg on which to begin to hang this story, admits to one tenuous, ridiculously thin and somewhat stretched link with the slightest out-of-the-normal: I was born and raised at Number Ten.

Thankfully, and I choose the word most deliberately, I refer to 10 Burnaby Road, not to that other slightly better known address recognised worldwide solely by its number. I was not born with a silver spoon in my mouth but, rather, was soon to be spoonfed considerable and regular servings of cods' liver oil and malt, which our family pet cat courted and cherished and appreciated much more than I did, but which I now admit, with considerable hindsight, must have helped to contribute to my still surviving. I weighed-in as a heavyweight in the upstairs front bedroom of Number 10 Burnaby Road, the ten-pound-seven-ounce third son of the former Miss Maud Charlotte Parker and second of her husband Joseph James Worsdale, police constable in the Southend County Borough Constabulary. Her firstborn, my late and much-loved half brother Peter, was fathered by a passing ship's steward in the night, when Maud was a teenager, but that is another story.

Ours was an old house, ours was, to pinch from some vintage song of which I know little else. It dated from the mid-Victorian period, give or take a year or two for argument's sake, if that's your attitude, and my dad paid about two-hundred pounds for it around 1930, on a mortgage from his own father, a jobbing builder and horse and cart lover. It was a few along from the start of the northern side of the street, in a terrace, with three downstairs rooms, plus a kind of forerunner of the conservatories of this age, except it was just a Jerry-built or Fred-built or even Joe-built leanto then. Embraced within the brickwork at the building's back corner, with a wooden door facing its counterpart nextdoor, behind the fence, was an outside lavatory with overhead cistern and chainpull. It was in the shaded area, never reached by direct sunlight, so it was not a place to linger even on warmer days, let alone cold nights, and not even with a hard-to-put-down book to continue or the day's paper to be read for news and entertainment long before we had telly.

There were three bedrooms upstairs. Part of the rear one was converted into a modern, indoor bathroom by my parents long after their sons had upped and gone on their own adventures and years ahead of mum and dad taking their own last journeys, within weeks of each other, after more than half a century of married life, almost all of it at this address. There had been other extensive modernisation improvements by then, too.

But we had no central heating, no modern conveniences, no indoor bathrooms, few comforts and the barest of necessities when my story began at Number Ten and through those opening chapters of my own life's tale. A tin bath that was kept on a hook on the backyard fence was carried into the kitchen, alongside the heated range, on Friday evenings for us boys' weekly soak and scrub. It took considerable strength and skill to carry away the water-filled container at the end of the oldest first, youngest last tub drill, without spilling any of the contents before reaching the backyard drainhole.

On our side of the road the houses were back-to-back with Beresford, a narrow alleyway separating the tiny backyards, occasional entryways between houses linking street to back alley, so that cycles could be wheeled in and out of rear gates and dustmen could call each week to collect the heavy, foul-smelling, stained and galvanised bins, then hump them on their shoulders to the roadside truck for emptying. On the other side of our street the house backed on to the cottages on Eastern Esplanade, the row of buildings that in turn faced across the open green on the seafront, which was developed into a putting course after the war. We had few of the luxuries or modern trappings and conveniences of the age, but we did have a grand community spirit. And we had our own tiny dairy at the corner of the street, run by the Porter family for decades before other owners came along years after I departed the scene. And we had the inevitable corner shop. The Gooding family ran it: old mum and dad, two sons, one daughter-in-law, I think. It was hardly big enough for more than half a dozen customers at most to squeeze in at any one time without suggestions of indecency, but it was sufficiently accommodating to need hired staff as well as all the family. Joan, from up the street, was appointed as an assistant when she left school and she stayed until she went and married a sailor after the war and sailed away to a new life in some unbelievably distant placed called Canada, where the policemen wore scouts' hats.

It seemed to offer everything, did Goodings. As my Dad used to say, "Soap, soda, starch, paraffin oil, a few old firelighters and a floating trunk from the Thames in the moonlight – it's all here." Well, almost everything. It even had its own little bakery department, in the charge of one of the two sons, while the other, named Percy, I think, delivered orders by motor van over great distances in those years long before supermarkets. The ovens were used on Christmas Days for cooking the turkeys of regular customers in and around our street, whose own stoves were far too small for the kinds of prize pluckers that were rare annual treats in times when the only takeaways anyone locally may have heard of, must have been robbers or pickpockets.

Just yards from Goodings' Aladdin's Cave of a store, on the opposite seafront corner of Burdett Road from the Army and Navy pub that became in turn all kinds of pubs and nightspots in later years, was Cleverly the butcher. Old Mr. Cleverly looked just as butchers ought to look: big and chubby and cheerful and rosily-pink of face, beefy of hands that held great knives and saws and cutters and which at the end of each day, wielded the scrapers and brushes that scrubbed and scoured the wooden blocks and benches spotlessly clean and white. Mr. Cleverly served all those wonderful things that were terribly bad for everyone who greatly appreciated them: hunks of suet as a main ingredient for pastry and puds, great blocks of beef dripping to be melted for the frying of chunky and fatty chips, pots of beef or pork dripping with delicious jellified gravy beneath, to be spread liberally on toast and sprinkled generously with salt, thick slices of brawn, thick belly of pork, rabbit pieces, pork chops containing the kidney – and, naturally, a penn'orth of pieces for the cat.

And then there was the fish. Oh, yes, the fish. Mother would tell a joke it took me quite a while and many repeats before I understood: "Take this money, go to the jetty and buy a pound of skates' eyeballs to see us through the week." Get it? Never mind. Forget it. But I still remember those eyeballs, those parts of the skate known by this description, and also the great wings of the fish, freshly caught and landed at the jetty that stuck out like a little landmark from that part of the prom which now traces the seaward edge of Adventure Island, the boating pool as was in my boyhood. We'd go with Mum, us boys, or on our own to buy from the gnarled and weatherbeaten and hardworking fishermen who brought their catches to the jetty, over whose sides great nets hung to dry or awaiting repair. Dabs, flounder, skate, plaice – flopping, flipping, flapping fish galore were there for the buying. And sprats. So many sprats, so cheap. A panful, sprinkled with salt, dry-fried whole was a teatime treat.

Tommy Nash supplied the shellfish: the whelks, mussels, winkles, cockles, crabs. He lived along our street, on the other side from us, where one of the entryways through the terrace reached his back garden and its shed, to which, presumably, his considerable supplies of goodies were delivered wholesale. Not too many people worried too much then about the likes of hygiene. Old Tommy piled high his ancient handcart with his assortment of offerings and toured the neighbourhood, his ringing handbell summoning the customers.

There were plenty of travelling tradesmen such as Tommy, familiar faces and favourites. In summertime open, flat-backed lorries from Garon's then so-advanced freezer and ice-making store behind premises at the High Street-Tylers Avenue junction, carried great blocks of ice on sacking sheets to various parts of town and to retail shops that had no facilities to make their own ice. Occasionally one of these trucks would trundle slowly through our neighbourhood. We would cling to the tailboard for a brief ride, little Tarzans swinging with the ease and daring of our hero Johnny Weissmuller, before dropping off at the next corner. Sometimes we would manage to snatch a piece of broken-off ice to suck. For those with pocket money, salesmen on Wall's Stop Me and Buy One trikes, chilled cabinet on wheels ahead of the handlebars, offered three-cornered ice-lollies in cardboard wrapping.

Laundry delivery vans came and went, too, to some homes. But ahead of the age of pushbutton convenience, before the modern electric washing machines, the weekly wash at Number Ten, as in most neighbouring homes and their like, was a laborious, time-consuming, ever-so-tiring routine. The whites and the coloureds among the items to be laundered, were separated. The whites were put in a huge copper of water and boiled for hours while being regularly prodded and pushed and stirred and agitated by a hand-held stick. The coloured items were hand-washed and rinsed. And everything, then, was put through a mangle, a handringer with two wooden or solid-rubber rollers that were turned by attached cast-iron handle, the squeezed-out water caught in a little tin bath beneath.

When the clothing had been wrung as dry as possible, it was hung on a high, outdoor line or, in winter, strung from the bars of what was known as a kitchen rack, a contraption familiar in the servants' quarters of major homes and popular in the terraces of Southend, too: a series of wooden rods, about six-feet in length, separated a few inches apart, in parallel, and slotted into decorative, wrought-iron endpieces. The whole thing, suspended on hooks from the ceiling, was raised and lowered by rope through a pulley.

So, on wet days and winter days, the laundry was dried indoors. Then, when the items had been smoothed with a solid flat-iron heated on the stove and lifted with a hand pad to avoid serious burns, they were draped again over the lowered rack, then raised so they would be aired by the rising warmth. Where there was a will – or a Maud or anyone else, come to that – there was as way.

We were smart and modern and ahead of the Joneses and other neighbours by the time I could note and remember my surroundings: we had mains electricity on our side of the street long before those on the other, for reasons I never fathomed. They had hissing gas lights with chalky-white mantels that blackened and charred under the naked flames and had often to be replaced. They had wireless sets fed by accumulator batteries, which had to be rented from Mr. Boitolt's garage. This was at the end of the unmade little lane off Burdett Road, immediately behind the Army and Navy pub, with a row of half-a-dozen cottages on the lefthand side before the whole immediate area was bulldozed in my time around those parts.

Mr. Boitolt, who always wore collarless shirts, black waistcoat and beaming smile, kept rows of thick-glassed accumulators on a long bench, stained by years of work and spilt oil and grease, that ran along the front wall of his garage-workshop, beneath windows grimed with dirt, so that the sun's afternoon rays from the west would hardly penetrate the dark interior. Few had private cars in my boyhood days behind The Mile, so Mr. Boitolt boosted his meagre income from motor repairs and servicing by looking after motor cycles and bicycles, mending punctures and, mainly, exchanging accumulators. There was considerable demand for these, for wireless was our link to the great world: a wonder of wonders.

We were terrified by the sinister voice of Valentine Dyall, the Man in Black, thrilled by the exploits of that great detective Paul Temple, and inspired by nightly episodes on the Light Programme of Special Agent Dick Barton and his sidekicks Jock and Snowy, when the only ever mention or suggestion or thought of something called sex was Middlesex, Sussex or Essex. We sat in ordered silence at teatime on winter Saturdays, while the football results were read in those crisp and plummy tones shared by every BBC announcer and our parents ticked-off their selections on the pools coupon, in ever-hopeful, ever-vain possibility that a fortune was on the way. We laughed at corny comics and listened to silken crooners and famous big hands and armed ourselves with pencils and paper to jot down the answers to quizzes.

And sometimes, just sometimes, we would be roused from our warm beds in the early hours, as a very special and so-daring treat, to join Dad in listening to crackling commentary from the other side of the Atlantic, when some British hopeful such as Farr or Cockell or Woodcock or Mills yet again became a brave, but battered and badly beaten hero of the boxing ring.

Raymond Glendenning and then, years later, Eamonn Andrews, painted such vivid word pictures for us, with W. Barrington Dalby, of the deep and doom-filled voice, giving what were called the inter-round summaries. Huddled round the wireless, wrapped in blankets, sipping hot cocoa, excited at our brief intrusion into this grown-up, nocturnal world, we visualised the smoke-filled and sweltering atmosphere in that distant land we knew from Hollywood films of Andy Hardy and Dagwood Bumstead and the like. We heard the fanfare for the entry of the gladiators, hometown hero cheered to the rafters, challenger from overseas booed or afforded grudging applause as another lamb being led to the slaughter. We heard the thuds and the blows and the roars of the bloodthirsty audience, appetites whetted and demanding yet another massacre inside the ropes. We could almost see what was being described, as the fighters ducked and bobbed, jabbed and weaved, clinched and clung on, desperate for the bell's ring and brief respite between rounds.

We knew, always knew, that time was fast running out for our man. "A good big 'un will always beat a good little 'un," said Barrington Dalby. And our good 'uns always seemed smaller than theirs, in the States. And so it would end, perhaps in a knockout, maybe through the referee's intervention when far too much punishment was being taken, at best having gone the distance, with the points tally favouring the hometown man. And so we would go to bed, remembering Dad's oft-repeated philosophy, 'The world loves a real trier, boys. Give of your best – that's all anyone can ask.'

2

IT was my wont to give of my very best, to try ever so hard, on the football field of play. I loved the game more than anything else, for quite a few years – until I fell for a way of working life I came to adore and then for a very special kind of girl, so that soccer slipped in my affections even if an affair with it has lasted still. That I did not become a star for Southend United and have the bigger clubs seeking my signature, was no mystery, however. Quite simply, try though I might – and I surely did – I was not naturally gifted and not naturally physically big and strong in the manner of the successful athletes, despite my arrival in the world as a bouncer. Well, I wasn't that much of a player, come right down to it.

Still, as the kind of trier about whom my dad often spoke, I persisted in playing the game of football with my mates from down by the Kursaal, at every opportunity, in street or in Southchurch Park or elsewhere, and I led them as a regular follower of the game at United's then Grainger Road Stadium, which years later was turned into a retail trading park, and occasionally on adventurous outings to see Tottenham Hotspur at White Hart Lane.

I earned my pocket money, from which to pay for admission to see the United and for the rare forays to the foreign parts of North London, on a daily paper round from the seafront shop, near the Kursaal corner, of the Godwins. The family, which played prominent and much-respected part in the Scout movement through many years and was involved in considerable charitable work, lived on the premises, I think, with a rear parlour and rooms upstairs. The little groundfloor frontage, in that short stretch between the Minerva and the Britannia pubs, some kind of food takeaway place in this age – what else? – was divided into a papershop immediately behind the central door off the footpath and a barber's tiny saloon to its rear, the domain of Sam, whom I imagined to be a survivor from the First War, with a gammy leg, pink face and snow-white hair. He attacked heads and shaved chins.

You couldn't, by any stretch of credibility, describe his surroundings as salon or hairdresser's. No, it was more sheep pen: a cramped, wooden-walled, box-like compartment with one chair for victims of Sam's shearing and a plank-like bench for those waiting their turn for tonsorial torture, while wondering whether to run for it before it was too late. A few nails and pegs protruded from the walls, just in case any customer wished to hang any garment while being short back and sided, or possibly even hang himself before submitting to haircut by a thousand nicks.

I was able truthfully to say that my dad had been a customer of another, nearby, barber since he first arrived in Southend from London in the early 1920s, to help to build a gasholder before becoming a copper, and my brothers and I always visited the same trimmer. Sam was not offended, far as I could tell, and I was mightily relieved.

My only fear was a meeting in the darkness of the Beresford Mansions with a man I was sure was the most terrifying screen Dracula of all time, Bela Lugosi. The block of flats had been built in 1913 by the Kursaal Estates company on the site of an old switch-back ride, as homes for staff. Now the apartments were rented to longstay tenants.

I had noticed this truly frightening man enter and leave the block on various occasions and I came to learn that he lived on the first floor and that I delivered a paper to his very door. His dark, slightly greying, hair began only about an inch above eyebrows of tangled barbed wire and was brushed back so that it thickly covered his head and hung deep on his neck. His face was sunken and sallow, his eyes like dark beads. I was convinced that if he parted his lips, he would reveal huge and sharp fangs. Thus, for more times than

I would be able to count, I crept quietly and slowly into the ground-floor hallway, mounted the stairs while holding my breath and close to fainting, and reached Dracula's landing with my heart thumping so loudly I was sure it must disturb anyone within a square mile. I would wait, trying to regulate the gasping, throat-constricting sound of my breathing, while slowly folding the paper sufficiently for it to enter the letter slot when I gently and ever-so-silently lifted the flap. And then I would strike the paper, so that it would zip like an arrow far into the hallway, and I would run back down the stairs and out of the door, fighting to gasp in some fresh air, desperately anxious to put space between myself and the Count.

We never did come face to face, Dracula's doppel-ganger and I, so I didn't tell the others about him. I went about my business of earning a few coppers and they went about theirs, collecting coke by the homemade barrow-load from the seafront gasworks to fuel the stoves and open fires of the local houses or running various errands.

In summer season, for a while, empty bottles on the beach provided a nice little earner. Many a daytripper or holidaymaker was in too lazy or carefree a mood to be bothered to return a lemonade bottle to nearby retailer and collect the penny deposit. Thus, for a boy such as me, trying to be a trier, opportunity knocked. I organised my mates into small groups, each taking a section of beach between Kursaal and Halfway House, which we considered our territory. Between us, we could gather dozens of empties from wastebins or simply discarded on the sands. Then, after giving the bottles a quick dip in the tide, we took it in turns, so we would not be so readily recognised, to take them to a shop along the Thorpe Bay seafront. The owner, busily preparing tea trays for beach customers or selling ice creams or buckets and spades, paid out the pennies and we later shared the spoils.

Such a venture into the capitalistic culture had to carry a risk, though. It was by pure bad luck that this one crashed the very day my turn arrived to take back the empties. There were rather a lot, actually: more than usual. So many, indeed, that we had put them in the boxed section of the four-wheeled, rope-pulled cart we had built long ago in Denny's backyard shed at the end of our road. This prized and shared possession was used for errands or for our own version of motor racing, zooming down the steep slopes of the cliffs just beyond the Calcutts pub at Westcliff, now the Esplanade, while trying to avoid trees and innocent passersby on the pavement below.

I pulled the cart to the doorway of the shop along the parade near Lifstan Way and announced to the man behind the counter, who for once was without customers and browsing through a paper, that I had twenty-six empties for him. This represented a fortune for me and my pals, but unfortunately the game was up.

"They're not my bottles – not from here," the man shouted angrily, coming from behind the counter. "I know your little game. You and your mates have been bringing lots of returns, haven't you? Well, that's it, no more money for you." Then came the real shock. As he neared, the red-faced man added, "You're a policeman's son, aren't you? I know your father -- he does duty along here. Just you wait; when I see him I'll tell him what you've been up to. Now clear off."

We returned the empties to a wastebin and closed this part of our business empire. It had not occurred to us that we had helped to clean up the environment and removed risk of broken glass and serious danger; and we had not thought we were doing anything too badly wrong, claiming money owed on empties, even though the filled bottles may not have come from where we returned them. I was well aware, though, that my father might not be amused. I lived in awful worry for a few days, resigning myself to trying to explain that I was only being a trier, trying to pay my way. But the matter was never mentioned and I never again went near that shop along the seafront. There would be some, today, who would say I had lost my bottle, but such sayings did not exist back then.

3

ONE of those customs that did exist back then, but has long since faded into insignificance beneath the sea of affluence and new money, was the penny-on-the-ball moneyraiser at professional football matches. Numbered tickets for a lucky – or, of course, unlucky – draw were offered at one old penny each to spectators immediately they had squeezed through the clickety turnstiles. The prize was the matchball as used that day. It was a considerable attraction, so one must assume that the ticket sales more than recouped for the football club the cost of the ball.

We talk here of far less complicated, much less sophisticated times, when football was a man's game, not women's, and when it was a working-class tradition handed down from grandfather to father to son, an escape from life's straitjacket on a Saturday afternoon, and never mind your fancy ideas of floodlit stuff and Sunday play and starting times dictated by billionaire media magnets. (Telly wasn't around much then, anyway, so the people's game remained mostly uncontaminated by greed). Only the nobs had seats; the rest of us, by far the greater number in crowds of at least several thousands, packed tightly on the terraces.

There were no Top of the Pops-type prematch programmes from in-stadium studios, hosted by raving disc jockeys, and no jumped-up, instant stars holding microphones and jigging up and down in the centre circle before kick-off. We stamped our feet and clapped our hands to the stirring, military music of uniformed, marching bands whose drum major sometimes caught the mace at first attempt when he tossed it into the air. This was pre-hamburger, pre-hotdog and all your fancy fayre: when a meat pie of mostly tough leather filling was hot enough to cause third-degree burns to the roof of the mouth and good enough for any boy because it had been good enough for dad. Pies survived for seasons – often the very same pies, it would appear.

This was also the era of blanket-carrying volunteers, who shuffled slowly round the perimeter of the playing pitch while the band played on, catching and collecting the coins thrown from the crowd in appreciation of the music. It was when the teams' members' names were chalked on a large board also carried round the runnning track – and when referees and linesmen were as deaf, blind, slow, dimwitted, crooked and as totally useless as they always had been and probably always would be.

And it was in this era, and at Grainger Road Stadium, which Southend United shared with a greyhound track, that I bought a winning ticket for the matchball draw. I had gambled one penny collected on an empty returned lemonade bottle from the man in the seafront shop who had committed me to a worrying wait lest he told my dad I had been up to no good. It was at halftime that the winning number was chalked in large letters on a board and carried round for public viewing.

I was standing on the shallow terracing, just behind the four-foot concrete perimeter wall, beyond which the dog track further distanced the spectators from the playing pitch, and I was at the northern end of the ground. This meant a long wait to know the number, the board being carried from the tunnel below the main west stand, then along the edge of the track on that side of the ground, to the south end and back up the eastern perimeter before finally and, agonisingly slowly, coming into my view. I searched my pockets for my ticket, in a frantic frenzy of fear that I might have lost it, for I was sure in my mind that the number on that board was the same as that on my little blue slip of paper. Oh, no, dear God, please don't let me have lost it. No, here it was, safe, and – yes – I held the winner. I was going to collect the ball used that very afternoon, kicked by the star players, no less; headed by that most courageous and awesome of centre-halves, that stopper of the notorious sliding tackle, old bullet bonce himself, Frank Sheard.

I clutched that ticket in my hand for the whole, ridiculously extra-long, forty-five minutes of a second-half in which my eyes seemed drawn to that ball like iron filings to a powerful magnet. When the final whistle blew, I hurried to where I must claim my prize, from a tiny office under the main stand.

It was a tee-ball, a leather sphere, each of whose many panels was shaped as a capital 'T'. It was slimy from the drizzle and mud, a scarred and scratched and gouged survivor from a battle, shining and new for the kick-off, aged and worn at the end like some veteran of conflicts galore. It was mine, a prize dreamed-off by countless others in that day's crowd in the manner of those of this age who conjure thoughts of winning the lottery or lifting some huge cheque from Chris Tarrant. Yes, it was mine – for one old penny and for years to come. What luck. What bliss. What joy. What a sensational day.

An unsmiling man at a little window, quite old, probably thirty or even forty, scrutinised the ticket I proudly handed to him, shaking with anticipation. He seemed to take forever before he reached below a shelf and handed to me the battered brown ball, still wet and mud-coated: "Ere y'are, son." It felt as heavy as a canonball.

I carried it home, the three friends with me pleading in turn for opportunity to hold it, to examine it, to count the scratches and the grooves, to wonder at its astonishing weight, to touch something that had been touched by the stars. Then I scrubbed it in the kitchen sink, watching the mud and the grit flow away, and I dried it best as possible with an old piece of rag before placing it close to the redhot kitchen range, which mother religiously blackened and polished early every day for a lifetime before relighting it to heat the water, warm the room, fire the oven in which she cooked our substantial, always tasty, if plain and simple and inexpensive, meals.

A woman of dedicated intent and exact routine, was Mum. Her second daily task after organising the kitchen range, summer and winter, in early daylight or darkness, was to polish the brass plate on the front doorstep and the brass fittings on the door. Such attention on the outside of the house, humble though the place might be in some eyes, was a signal of cleanliness and tidiness and orderliness inside, too.

When the ball lying in front of the range finally felt fully dry to the touch, I took it out to the tiny shed in the backyard, where my father had a small workbench, shelves full of odds and ends and near-empty, rusting paint tins and the foot last and tools he used to resole our boots and shoes. There, ball on bench, a treasure to be studied and sighed over yet again, I smeared it liberally with dubbin from a tin as slippery from use on football boots as the Artful Dodger. It added a shining lustre to my prized possession and would help to protect it from the wet and the mud that awaited it early next day. The kids from Burnaby and Beresford and various streets within strolling distance of Southchurch Park would recreate the match as played that Saturday by our Southend United heroes.

I palmed great, thick splodges of dubbin over every panel, caressing and fondling the ball like some elderly Romeo with a new young love, working the protective grease into the stitched seams and into the leather lace, so that the ball could have slipped from the hands like opportunity, except that there was no way I would willingly release it.

I took it with me to my little bedroom that night and placed it on an old, folded newspaper, so that I could see it once more as I reached to turn out the light and see it again immediately I opened my eyes in the early daylight. It was beyond compare. And when I took it later that morning to the park, word spread that the boy with the ball this day, for we turned up in numbers never knowing whether anyone would actually possess a football for a game; the boy with a proper, real, leather, full-sized ball, had won it the previous afternoon, for just a penny. And it had been used in the real, live match by the real, live professionals. And now, here it was, all clean and dubbined and being allowed to be used again. There was unusual rush over the choosing of sides from the mob of potential participants and a hurried marking-out of the playing pitch with piles of clothing heaped at the paced-out four corners and yet more belongings in small mounds to identify the two goals. We did not enjoy the luxury of a proper pitch with corner flags and goalposts and nets and all that kind of thing. Not everyone had football boots, either. But imagination can sketch almost anything in young minds; draw the shapes and the lines where they ought to be and where they would be, anyway, if there were a groundsman to pre-prepare everything.

The ball that everyone was anxious to kick, was placed in the nominal, sort of paced-out centre of this makeshift pitch and the sides lined-up, twelve-year-olds confidently certain they would in time turn out for Southend United, if not for England. This fixture, however, was between The Shirts and The Skins – those with some kind of top, any kind of top, above their shorts or their trousers, and those bare from the waist upwards and desperately anxious to start play before succumbing to frostbite.

A pink-faced, ever-smiling and chubby boy with protruding teeth as black and uneven as a breakwater across the road and on the beach, was centre-forward for the team of which I was captain and goalie. His name, I seem to recall, was Cuthbert, though for some reason he begged and demanded to be known as Bert. As it was my ball, I had picked the teams and I would shout the moment for kick-off, since a whistle was also something we did not possess and there was no referee. I yelled and Bert booted the ball with all his might. "Bloody hell's sodding bells," he screamed, as he fell over, clutching at his right foot. "It's not a ball, it's a bleedin' boulder. I've broken my ankle."

He was exaggerating, of course. Play had started, in any case. So no one took any notice of the writhing Bert. Like a mob chasing a pickpocket, the crowd of kids, The Skins and The Shirts, scrambled after the ball that had travelled all of five or six feet after Bert's baptismal boot. He crawled to the edge of the playing area, rubbing his ankle and cursing loudly until he was unable any longer to ignore being ignored and hurried to rejoin the fray. Then, bustling through the crowd, his bulk easily brushing aside those who tried to tackle him, he bore down on the goal and hit the lethal ball straight towards a terrified little goalie guarding the space between the two piles of clothing. The custodian managed apparently quite easily to catch the ball, much to his own considerable surprise and relief. Alas for him, though, its eel-like quality, thanks to my generous application of dubbin, saw it slip from his grasp and over the line. The Skins leapt up and down as warriors, roaring, Goal! Great goal!

Bert turned to accept the congratulations of his teammates and The Shirts said it was all a bloody fix and in any case, the ball was beyond any regulation weight and cheats never prospered and if it had been a proper ball the goalie would have saved it and Bert had left the pitch and come back on only when the play was near the opponents' goal and it wasn't fair. And so on.

I said it was a real, proper, regulation, professional ball that had been used by Southend United in their two-nil win over Reading in the Third Division (South) yesterday and that was good enough for me and for anyone else who wanted to continue to play for The Skins or The Shirts. Cuthbert said I was right, because it was my ball and if I hadn't brought it along there'd be no match, anyway, and so we got on with the game.

We played with the ball again, many times. All of us began to kick it harder and for longer distances and we even headed it when, at first, we had felt that its considerable weight would drive us into the soft ground like nails thumped home by heavy hammer. It survived several long winters and lashings of dubbin until its stitches began to burst and the inner bladder poked out pink and rude and grotesque and not at all nice. And what finally became of it, I simply cannot remember.

It disappeared from my orbit, as did Cuthbert and all those of The Skins and The Shirts and as did leather footballs when poncy white plastic ones were introduced and as did leather ankle boots with steel-lined toecaps when fancy-dancy pumps were donned by Maradonnas and prima donnas of modern-age football. If Bert, who was Cuthbert, is still around, I can well imagine him saying of today's millions of midget Beckhams playing in public parks, while their mums and dads swear and fight each other on the touchline, "Bloody twerps. Don't even know what day it is."

4

SOME of those who met up in the park, to run and jump and skip; to hide and to seek through the thirty or so green and pleasant acres; to chase around or simply to sail model boats on the little lake, were pupils at Thorpe School, in Greenways. It was a modern building, part of the 1930s development of the eastern edge of Southend at Thorpe Bay, where the boundary crept ever closer to Shoebury, which had been enfolded by the arms of municipal Southend in 1933 and pressed to the county borough breast in what some thought obscene and objectionable, but had to accept.

Greenways was a posh school in a posh place, as viewed by the rest of us, the majority from our little community clustered down by the Kursaal and the seafront. My parents had longed to buy one of the new semis at the edge of the new suburbia of that last decade ahead of war, in the new Lifstan Way, beyond which lay mostly fields and then the centuries-old Thorpe Hall, a former manor, and its modern golf club. But at asking prices around four-hundred pounds, such houses were far too expensive – at least twice what Number Ten might fetch. And so, with my friends from the immediate neighbourhood, I went to Brewery Road School, at the top of Southchurch Avenue, just over the rail bridge.

Brewery Road had opened in 1892, when the town was first reaching out in any substantial manner east of the High Street. By the time the likes of me sat at one of its little wooden desks and began to dip pen nib into ink well, there was a kind of double layer of pupils: the children of the more permanent of residents in and around the Kursaal and the Golden Mile area and the terraced roads packed between there and Southchurch Road, who attended the year round; and those from the itinerant families of seasonal workers who arrived at Easter, stayed until October in rooms or shared lodgings, filling a variety of jobs, then disappeared come winter. Against no little odds, good discipline was maintained amid what seemed to me considerable kindness and happiness; but educational standards naturally varied considerably.

Brewery Road was well beyond its half-century, a redbrick building with a tiny tarred-over playground and not a blade of grass in immediate sight, when those with powers to make changes, decided that a change of name would help its image. It became Porters Grange, named after the nearby late 15th or 16th century manor house, taken over by the town as the civic house and mayoral parlour in 1935, the delightful focal point of an area known as Porters Town in the infancy of the modern Southend. The school did very well, thank you, under a series of head teachers on the way to its centenary and beyond. Mind you, that was long, long after I and others of the more permanent of locals had moved to Southchurch Hall, that big and daunting elementary school that opened in 1904 opposite the rail line in Ambleside Drive and is now an adult community education centre.

By the time of my arrival as a pupil, Southchurch Hall was well and truly under the considerable influence and command of the redoubtable headmaster Wellesley Haxell, who bucked no nonsense, though he had a golden heart and caring demeanour, and the likes of Mr. Lewis, the woodwork master, who would creep up behind any mischievous boy – boys such as me, of course – and whack 'em on backside or back of hand with a wooden rule.

Our class teacher, whom I shall remember as Old Ted for the sake of this true tale, also taught science in the lab where I managed once to knock over a Bunsen burner, by pure accident, so that some nearby methylated spirit burst into flame and raced along a bench top before the blaze was extinguished. The incident left a great, blackened area as a reminder when I returned to the building years later, to attend evening classes and to wander briefly back into boyhood in corridors and rooms that once echoed with the wonderful sounds of the young.

Teacher Ted used to light a cigarette, pour himself a cup of coffee from a flask, and tip back in his chair, feet on desk, when he dispatched us to the playground for morning break. He once quietly invited a pal and I to Saturday afternoon tea. We were proud to be chosen, my own parents most impressed. We went to Ted's house in a little road off Victoria Avenue. He opened the front door, invited us into the hallway, where his drop-handled bicycle leaned against a wall, and led us to a back room, where he smilingly and enthusiastically encouraged us to drink orange cordial and select from a plate of meat paste sandwiches and another of iced cakes.

Then he said he thought it would be wonderful fun if we played a game called Murder in the Dark. He would pull all the downstairs curtains together and we would go to the front room to hide and he would come to find us. We almost did as we were told; except that when we went into the hall and Ted began loudly to count to ten in the backroom, we quietly opened the front door, went out, closed it behind us and strolled all the way home. We said we had had a lovely time and the day was never mentioned again, not even on the Monday, when we were back at school and Old Ted, who was probably in his mid-thirties, was behind his usual desk with his usual casual manner.

I did well at this school, always in the top three or four in most subjects, so that when time arrived to sit the scholarship exam, later known as the eleven-plus, I passed. I was offered a place at Southend High School and my proud parents bought me a restored, secondhand bike from the Tunbridge Road Cycle Stores, so I would pedal the three miles or so each morning from home down by the Kursaal. I went up through the backstreets to Southchurch Road and then along Prittlewell Path from its start at Milton Street to its end near Prittlewell station, in East Street. Then I continued to the St. Mary's junction, down the hill, and into Fairfax Drive and Prittlewell Chase. I usually returned home by slightly different route, just to vary the pattern, cycling the length of the then beautiful, tree-lined

Victoria Avenue, with its grand detached homes on either side. They hadn't brought in the planners and the indiscriminate wreckers of the town by then: such civic and legalised vandalism as would be schemed and agreed in Town Hall, had not even been dreamed of – it was years into a future none could have foreseen. So I pedalled from Earls Hall Avenue, at the end of which the historic building that lent its name to the road, was still just standing before it, too, was consigned to oblivion.

I made my steady way along the avenue, up the steep hill to where there still were shops on the southeast corner of the junction, across from the Blue Boar, and along the lovely road that had long since linked Prittlewell with the fledgling Southend. I recall many fine houses and on the west side, to my right, as I pedalled homewards, there was the private Clark's College. The ugly sixties would bring the towering Civic Centre, the new police station and the kinds of highrise office blocks and dominant, concrete and glass structures seen so far only at the cinema.

There were options of route at Victoria Circus, where a tall policeman – often my own father – directed the traffic. There was a left turn into Southchurch Road, right turn to London Road, or straight ahead and into The Broadway, as we knew the top end of High Street. This was my usual choice: to pedal slowly through a packed and teeming, so-alive main shopping street because, at its end, I could freewheel down the steep hill mysteriously holding the official name Royal Hill, but never to my knowledge known as or referred to, as other than Pier Hill.

I never failed but to appreciate the view to my right, of the Pier itself and the Thames and, half-right, that magnificent, sweeping canvas of the estuary and the distant hills of Sheppey and Kent: an ever-changing, always magnetic backdrop. Best of all, though, as a young boy, was the sense of speed and power and freedom as one soared down that long incline, able to progress far along Marine Parade before the need for a little gentle pedal power to complete the journey home. Of course, this was years before Marine Parade – or, rather, the so-called traffic calmers – gave motorists the hump. I never minded the long cycle ride; not even when it was raining heavily and I wore a waterproofed hat and yellow oilskin cape that was buttoned tightly round the neck and hung like a belltent, covering my own frame and that of the machine, with its modern, three-speed gear change. Yet I was ever reluctant to set off in the mornings and desperately longed to be on the return journey in the afternoon. For I hated being a pupil at Southend High, from first to last. These schooldays were not the best days of my life; they were the worst.

It was a time of intense frustration and sadness, of immense despair. Rightly, wrongly, foolishly, unnecessarily or understandably, I felt like an outcast. I looked upon the headmaster, Dr. William Isaac Moore, known to generations of boys as Plug, for some reason I have never established, as a snob. Now, this may seem a cruel and improper observation, at this considerable distance of time, and when one acknowledges that Dr. Moore served his school and Southend with great distinction and recognition for more than two decades from 1929, including overseeing the move from the town centre building to the new complex at Prittlewell Chase just ahead of the war, whose end was approaching when I became a pupil.

Possibly I was overwhelmed by the fine progress of my older brother, three years ahead of me at the school and with many friends who seemed to this eleven-year-old newboy to be so clever; or maybe I was much in awe of the tales of those of past generations of pupils who had gone on to become famous figures in so many different fields and in so many parts of the world. Perhaps I was unduly sad and lonely at being the one and only youngster from my part of the town to win a place, so that I personally knew no one when I arrived at the school and had no contact with any of the others of my year at the end of each day or at weekends.

But what most affected me, a desperately-lonely boy among so many strangers and so many academic achievers, was that somehow, some way, through some attitudes or passing remarks I simply cannot now recall, I was made to feel a subject of snobbery: a boy from a terraced street, from a working class family and a working class neighbourhood. Utterly and completely ridiculous in this age, of course; but not untypical of that time, in the 1940s, when class distinctions were marked, all BBC radio announcers spoke as ever-so-wonderfully correct and decent chaps and gals and even supposedly Cockney characters on the silver screen were from the Rank charm school. I had not personally experienced the feeling I now had; and it cut, deeply.

Years later, a man who was of a school generation immediately ahead of mine and who went on to gain considerable educational honours and to establish a successful private and public life in Essex, said to me one day, without the slightest prompting, "You went to Southend High, didn't you? Plug Moore was head in your time, too, wasn't he? Snob, wasn't he? Awful snob. I won a school prize on one occasion and was called to the stage in front of a packed hall and many visitors. Plug asked me out loud, 'And what do you propose to do, young man?' I said I wanted to be an engineer. Plug looked slowly at me, then turned to the audience and said with a slight smile, 'Engineer? Engineer? Did you hear that, ladies and gentlemen? This young man wants to be an engineer.' I went red, felt totally humiliated, thanked the head for my book and walked back to my seat. I never, ever forgot that occasion."

I would not forget my years under the eye of Dr. Moore, either. I felt out of place and I counted every lesson every single day, desperately anxious for it to end. I yearned for the arrival of every weekend, then gradually dreaded the inevitable approach of Monday morning. I slipped into the lower classes and was not even in the top few of those. I daydreamed during lessons, of maybe going to sea, of becoming a great footballer, of playing in a band as a drummer; above all, of finding some reason to get away from school when, in my earlier years, I had loved school and enjoyed every day. And so it came that I fell foul of Dr. Moore and he caned me. I probably deserved what I got, within the rules that then applied in schools.

I was ordered to his study. I walked along the polished, wood-blocked floor of the long, otherwise empty main east-west corridor one afternoon, the sun throwing beams of light through the tall, glass-panelled doors beyond which a tree-lined avenue to the main gates and freedom briefly tempted me to run away, a notion quickly dismissed. I tapped on the head's door and was summoned before the bald-headed man, a short figure with thin lips and thin-rimmed spectacles, aged then in his mid-fifties. I cannot remember what he said, except that I was disobedient and a disappointment and would have to be taught a lesson.

Then he went to select from several long and thin canes that stood in a cylindrical container in the corner of the room, one that he carefully and slowly bent and straightened and tested while at the same time peering silently at me and prolonging the agony ahead. He then ordered me to lean across the edge of his desk and be raised the cane and brought it down in a series of whipping, lashing strikes across the seat of my short, grey trousers. The pain was excruciating. I think he hit me six times, but no longer can recall.

When he had finished administering this punishment that was to teach me right from wrong and turn me into a good boy, he told me to stand up. The pain was such that I found it extremely difficult to rise from the bent position, but I did so and I looked straight at Dr. Moore, not a tear in my eyes, though I wanted badly, so badly, to cry with hurt and anger. "Let that be a lesson to you. Go back to your classroom," he said.

"Thank you, sir," I said, forcing the slightest of smiles of sheer defiance. "Thank you very much." I left and walked slowly and in extreme pain back along the corridor to the classroom. I was proud of myself, for I had not shown any kind of emotion to Dr. Moore and not shed one tear. I tapped on the classroom door, was ordered to enter and told to return to my seat. When I sat down the pain was almost beyond belief, the searing sensation so sharp that I almost shouted out aloud. But I gripped the edge of the desk and forced myself to sit still, until the hurt slowly eased.

I never told my parents of that caning or of other punishments, of the hundreds of lines I had to write, repeating that I must not daydream in class or must pay more attention. I even devised a method of holding three pens at one time, the nib of the second in the trio slightly beyond the first, the third protruding downwards a little beyond the second, so that a sloping effect of the nibs allowed me to scribble three identical lines at a time.

My mother and father could not understand why my academic standards had fallen, why I had slipped so far from those top few places I always occupied at the unfashionable Brewery Road and Southchurch Hall schools and why my reports in most subjects from Southend High inevitably carried remarks that I could do better, needed to pay much more attention, was capable of much more than I ever achieved. Where others before and since did so well at Southend High and where they have fared so well and have so much and so many to recall with fondness and gratitude, I looked back on my four years with intense regret and wonderful relief when finally they were behind me.

Yet, as ever in life, there always was and always is something to be gained among the losses. I became independent and determined and a survivor and I told myself that the four years at one school was but a tiny one of those fractions I never easily or successfully mastered at lessons. Challenges and chances lay ahead.

And I was right. I applied for and was given a job at the old Southend Standard publishing company by a gruff, no-nonsense, yet lovely man named Bert King, the works manager. I had turned fifteen years old in the April and, when the summer holidays arrived in the July, I saw the vacancy advertised in the Thursday Standard while my parents were on a week's visit to relatives and I was staying with neighbours. I went to the Cliff Town Road works and offices, was interviewed in a tiny, glass-walled office at the foot of the stairs, and was so enthusiastic, so keen, so willing to do whatever might be required of me in the line of duty – running errands, sweeping-up the debris from parcel-packing on Wednesday press nights, getting the printers' cheese rolls and fags for morning break, being a copyholder for the experienced proof readers – I was offered the job. I would start two weeks later, at eight on a Monday morning, cycle to be left in a rack in a corrugated-roofed shelter in a backyard off the alleyway that separated Cliff Town and Weston Roads. I would be paid twenty-five shillings a week. I could not imagine anything more wonderful, more motivating, more rewarding – anything more utterly, truly, fantastically wonderful than never, ever going back through the door of the school and proving to myself and to anyone else who might care, that I was bright, industrious, determined. I needed these attributes, as well as considerable pleading and praying, to convince my mother and father, the moment they returned home, to allow me to take up the job I had already accepted. Rarely, if ever, would any firm have a more willing, enthusiastic and dedicated apprentice. Life was great, especially great, at that moment.

5

I'D had a taste of working for a living a year or two before I escaped from my private hell at school, if only in a part-time, temporary way, and I had enjoyed it as I would in later life appreciate nice food and wine, books and music. I became a workaholic as a boy and I remain so, well beyond that artificial barrier of advanced age.

In my summer holidays, when the war was over and the men came home with their cash gratuities and life was never again going to be the same, for good or bad; and when the women were released temporarily from their inhibitions and their struggles to survive, I became ticket boy on the jockey scales outside the main entrance to the Kursaal. They were owned by Old Bill, our neighbour. He had another set along Western Esplanade, opposite the Alexandra Yacht Club, which he rented out on franchise.

This set, like those where I spent long hours each day of the holidays, were vintage scales of gleaming brass with studded leather chair suspended on one end of the high cross bar, the other end balanced by a flat pan below chains to each of its corners. A pile of different-sized iron weights, ranging from half an ounce to one stone, were close by, so that the scales' operator could speedily heap on to the pan more or less sufficient to match the weight of a customer seated in the chair.

My job was to steady the chair, standing close behind it, while the scale man, sitting on a tiny stool and bending forward, hefted the weights on to the pan. There were, even then, Jack-the-Lads who reckoned they could crash heavily backwards into the chair, so that the weights lifter would be caught unawares, maybe even caught under the chin by the fast-rising pan. But no one ever caught Old Bill in this way, and he was the operator most days, handing over only occasionally and briefly to a part-timer while he had a break or, more likely, popped into the nearby Minerva or one of the other Golden Mile pubs for a "livener."

Old Bill was of retirement age when I worked alongside him, a neat and tidy man from an earlier age, who wore suspenders over the insteps of his shoes, favoured starched white collars and silk ties and only removed his jacket, while still retaining his waistcoat, on the hottest of days. He was a toff, to look at, and a man of impeccable manners and soft politeness of speech, given to saying he had had elegant sufficiency, thank you, whenever he completed a meal cooked by my mother.

Unflappable behind the array of weights, as might well be expected of a man who spent his winter months as a part-time clerk with the Electricity Company, keeping the books in meticulous handwriting, Old Bill would lean towards the pan, quickly glance at the next customer and speed the weights into place, never needing more than the tiniest of them all, the half-ounce, to complete a perfect match. He hardly moved his head: just his eyes, to weigh-up the next in line, and then his hands as he dealt the weights with the dexterity of a card sharp.

When the customer in the suspended chair and the weights were exactly balanced and matched, Old Bill would call out the figures and I jotted them with a thick, lead pencil on the next tear-off ticket on the pad. His cool and calculated performance, lifting and moving those weights for hours on end, a small, balding and slim man whose lower arms beneath his rolled-to-the-elbows shirt sleeves, were muscular and criss-crossed with bulging veins, drew large crowds. It was easy to see or hear someone in the mob challenge another to jump backwards into the chair, to try to trick Old Bill, but he was always ahead of them, uncannily so.

There were days when Bill seldom had a break and when I handed over tickets galore after first collecting the threepence fee. The old bronze threepenny coins or coppers were dropped into a tall, slim box next to Bill. At some time in a day, when finally he had a brief rest, he would tip the contents into money bags that few others would be able to lift, then he would effortlessly carry it to the counting house inside the Kursaal, where he was fond also of dallying for a Guinness or a few. The great amusement arcade and grounds dealt always in cash in those years, of course: vast mountains of cash. So Bill's change, considerable in itself, was small by comparison and he was given notes in exchange.

Larry Gains, a great heavyweight boxer ahead of the war, a much-admired and skilful fighter born in 1900 in a tough part of Toronto, an imposing man who had won the Canadian and British Empire titles and beaten some of the world's greats such as Max Schmelling and Primo Carnera during a long career, was a regular customer. Some six-feet-three or more, muscular and powerful still, not an ounce of spare weight on his 15-stone or so frame, he would politely exchange conversation with Old Bill, then sit gently in the chair. "Same, Larry – just the same as yesterday," Old Bill would say. I didn't have to write a ticket; Larry knew his weight and needed no reminder. "Thanks, Bill," he'd say. And to me, "Thanks, son."

It didn't occur to me then, as such a young lad, that this once-great fighter, this handsome, dark-complexioned man who had thrilled countless thousands and battled with the best in the world, in those sadly and disgracefully intolerant and divisive times, had ended up where so many of his kind and his courage finally came to rest after their careers were over. He was low in the scheme of things, while the hangers-on had found other pegs. Larry had a little band and he played the drums and helped to draw the crowds to the Minnie pub, because they wanted to see the man who had been a king of the ring. He had a reputation as a gentleman and gentle giant and great sportsman.

The last I heard of Larry, he was steward of a working men's club in Shoebury and he committed some misdemeanour, put one mark on his blameless record, and fell foul of the law and then fell from public view. He moved away and, I believe, died when he was eighty-three. He was one of many characters along and around the Golden Mile in that era. Happy Harry was the most famous, of course. There's a tiny plaque on the seawall, opposite the historic Hope Hotel, fairly close to the Golden Mile pitch where he preached, or perhaps performed, through fifty summers and more before, in the mid-1970s, ill health finally forced him to admit his years of ministry to the mobs and the masses were over. He was 86 when he died – though he had already seemed ancient to me, as a boy, when first I was mesmerised and mystified so that I could spend hours among the crowds surrounding him in a great circle, several deep, for his "services." Was he a True Believer? Or a charlatan? Or simply an eccentric? A bit of each, I suspect.

In those postwar summers when Southend was packed as never before or since; when hundreds of thousands poured out of the rail stations and the charabanc parks as lava from a highly-active volcano, Happy Harry, whom few knew to be the Pastor George Woods, originally from South London, was one of the truly great characters the trippers wanted to see and hear. His reputation had grown since the previous war. Generations had spread the news of his performances, often considerably embellished, as he himself held court to spread the word of the Lord (and to raise a few bob, quite a few bob, to help to finance the spreading of that word).

Slightly cross-eyed behind thick-lensed, steel-rimmed specs, a shock of wild grey hair floating from a suntanned scalp, Happy Harry, a featherweight figure in starched white dog collar, black suit and black boots, suffered considerably for his beliefs. He was jokingly challenged and chivvied, taunted and harangued. He parried the verbal attacks, exchanging good-natured banter and commending his tormentors to heed the words he read from the Bible or recited from memory. But sometimes he was physically assaulted. He would recall being stabbed with pins, pelted with rubbish, having lighted paper pinned to the tail of his coat, being thrown into the sea.

I watched him for hours as he smiled through the ridicule, won over those who would recite prayers or sing hymns with him, commanded sinners to admit their wrongs and to change their ways.

Rascal, rogue or truly religious, Happy Harry attracted and held his audiences as only the greatest of performers can, rarely failing to smile, his face and hands weather-beaten, he himself never defeated. And at the end of each service, or performance, before he took a brief break and then began all over again, Harry invited his listeners to contribute, if they would be so kind, to God's work. He would sing a song that I often joined in singing out loudly and with wild and exaggerated enthusiasm, as did so many of his regulars in the crowds: It's rolling in, it's rolling in, the sea of love is rolling in. And I believe, and I receive, the sea of love is rolling in.

The money did roll in, too. A few of the more unruly threw coins at Harry, so there were times when he was badly bruised on face or hands. Some louts even gripped the edges of large old pennies while heating the other edges with a cigarette lighter, so that when the coins were thrown and Harry reached for them, his fingers were burned. Through it all, though; through the verbal and physical violence, there was almost always a considerable majority who appreciated the lengthy and free show by a rare character whose contribution to the popularity and growth of Southend was recognised only long after his death and only by a handful of volunteers of the Southend Society, a group of lovers of the town's past.

When each service had ended, when the last notes of It's Rolling In faded and the crowds began to drift away, Harry would gather the coins from the ground; the halfpennies, pennies, three-penny bits, sixpences if lucky. The occasional glint of silver was seen amid the considerable copper. I can recall more than once noticing Harry late on summer evenings, when the masses had mostly gone, sitting over a pint in a window seat of the seafront Falcon pub, counting coins. By then, I believe, he owned a house in Leigh, but he is said to have ended his years in an old folk's residential home back in his South London surroundings, from where he was called to glory.

AND then, of course, there was Tornado. George Smith, extrovert entertainer, daredevil eccentric, Wizard of the Wall, stuntman and showman supreme. The man who rode the Wall of Death in the Kursaal for some four decades until he retired and sold up, a few years before his death in 1972, was another whose fame pulled-in the crowds with the success of a championship tug-of-war team.

His exploits and his reputation were handed down through generations from the dawn of the 1930s to the late 1960s. Unlike Happy Harry, Tornado Smith was never recognised with any permanent plaque or memorial in his name and honour in or by the town where he made his own fame and fortune while contributing immeasurably to the astonishing success of the seaside resort. Indeed, it was not until the autumn of 1999, nearing the end of a century in which Tornado Smith was such a unique character, that he was officially remembered in Boxford, the north Essex village of his boyhood, where he began riding motorcycles and started to develop his skills and perfecting his trickery.

Huge crowds turned out to witness the unveiling of an English Heritage blue plaque. But the occasion merited little attention in Southend, where there seems considerable reluctance at any civic level to acknowledge and accept that the town's reputation, survival, growth and considerable triumphs as a resort owed much to the likes of plain Mr Smith.

He is clearly remembered by the writer of this journal, though. Growing up close to the Kursaal in the 1930s, living mere yards from the then twenty-acre amusement park behind the famous domed frontage, ballroom, offices and arcade until into the 1950s, one could hardly escape the sound of revving motorcycles as they were ridden by Tornado and a succession of young men and women assistants and co-riders, round the cylindrical Wall of Death on summer days and well into summer evenings. Many times I was among those who climbed the steps to squeeze onto the platform that encircled the Wall near its top, so that the spectators, all standing, all craning forwards for a better view, looked down as the performers first circled the bowl-shaped base, then slowly rode up the sheer wooden sides of the structure, in corkscrew fashion, to where, at their highest level, they were mere inches from the viewers' faces. The shaking and shuddering of the wall's tall panels, the exaggerated noise from the engines inside the drum-like structure, the smell of the machines' fuel and oil, the screams and then thunderous applause from the crowd – they can be recalled and recaptured even now, if one closes one's eyes and concentrates on that time long gone.

George Smith, who would became the famous Tornado, began his working life as one of those motorcycle patrolmen for a motoring organisation in the 1920s, when private cars were appearing more frequently on the roads. Clearly, such a sedate and orderly way of life, travelling the roads around the East Coast seaside town of Clacton, saluting passing motorists and endeavouring to help those in trouble, was not quite what the young Mr. Smith wanted from life. He had already perfected some tricks on two wheels and obviously was not lacking in courage; so he went off to South Wales, to ride the Wall of Death at Barry. Before long, he felt that a return to Essex, and especially to the booming Southend, would pay handsomely. He was correct.

He opened a Wall in the Kursaal, yet another innovative attraction for a great amusements park, a forerunner of the much later theme parks, always boasting new crowd-pulling features from many parts of the world. Tornado packed 'em in, for show after show, every day through the long summer seasons in the truly heady years leading up to the war and then again after it. He rode solo, sometimes sitting with his back to the handlebars, arms stretched behind him. He carried an assistant on pillion, usually an attractive young woman who stood, arms raised, while machine and riders apparently defied gravity and never showed any suggestion of fear. He developed a stunt where he and two others performed a triple weave as they circled the wall, the spectators surely more nervous than the riders, terrified some awful accident must occur. And he at one time also included a lion in his act. The advertised great beast, a truly frightening king of the jungle, was a toothless, aged and trained, somewhat tame animal that sat placidly on the petrol tank of Tornado's bike as they rose and dipped, round and round the walls;

but how were the paying customers to know? At the end of each show, just before the crowd filed out, to be replaced within minutes by another, Tornado would appealingly and so convincingly explain that because of the extreme dangers, he and his fellow performers could never, ever get insurance, not at any price. Thus, any contributions beyond the entrance fee, would be warmly welcomed. For Tornado, as for Happy Harry, across the other side of the Golden Mile, the sea of love came rolling in: the coins were showered to the Wall's wooden-planked floor from the people above.

Tornado and his assistants collected the money as quickly as possible before the next show began. At night, when the last of the shows had ended and the trippers or holidaymakers had headed for their charabancs, trains or boarding houses, Tornado crawled beneath the flooring to search for every halfpenny or penny that had slipped between the planks. He was said by some, in later years, to be as tight as a shirt collar two sizes too small; and to have amassed a fortune before he retired to some distant place in the sunshine. Fact and fiction merged long before then; and since he encouraged publicity and pulled many stunts aimed at attracting it, separating truth from myth was very difficult.

It is known that he rode a penny-farthing cycle around the town; I often saw him, almost always dressed in black beret, white shirt with dark tie, black riding jodhpurs and knee-length, gleaming black leather riding boots. It is true, too, that in the early postwar years he was found guilty of some minor motoring offence and was fined. He pedalled to the courthouse behind the Victorian police station in Alexandra Street, which was later demolished to create a car park, parked his bicycle outside and, when ordered to pay the fine, tipped a bag of farthings on to the clerk's desk.

It made wonderful copy for the reporters representing the daily papers, as many successful journalists did in those years of a bustling and thriving town ahead of television. It added up to the kind of wide publicity that Tornado had undoubtedly anticipated, at a fraction of the cost of any advertising and surely with more far-reaching impact than any paid space could have had. As successive generations of visitors to Southend looked down on Tornado from their paid places on the high platform, so there naturally would be those then, and since, who would look down on any such vulgar and common, mass-appeal attractions as a Wall of Death. But George Smith, showman extraordinary, was part of a town and a time of immense success. Somehow, his likes are not around any more.

6

THERE were many characters in our neck of the woods, when I was a boy. They did not have the kind of fame or notoriety or hero-worship of a Happy Harry or a Tornado Smith; and they would not have been well known outside their own immediate surroundings. For Southend was then as it is now: many different and distinct hamlets and villages of varying appearances, reputations, conditions and residents, all embraced within a borough born officially in 1892, re-christened as a county borough in 1914 and considerably enlarged in this relatively brief timescale by the additions of Southchurch, Leigh, chunks of Eastwood and the whole of Shoebury.

Down our way, in our tiny corner, the visiting tens of thousands arrived and departed in summer from the huge charabanc park on the south of the Kursaal grounds. This ran the length of Beresford Road, from behind the great stage of the wonderful Ballroom building to Arnold Avenue and was perhaps one-hundred yards deep, to where it disappeared in the shadow of the enormous Cyclone Railway, a fist-clenching, stomach-raising, heart-stopping, scream-provoking rollcoaster that soared to considerable heights and plunged to great depths as the mile-long track twisted and turned through its intricate, complicated, jigsaw of a mighty wooden structure.

The strangers of summer, the unknowns to us, had their own considerable characters who donned fancy hats, blew mouth organs and penny whistles, squeezed piano accordions or willing women, sang and danced, drank and dined, paddled in the briny, shoes and socks removed, trousers rolled knee-high to reveal snow-white legs, sauteed under the sun, meandered along the Mile, promenaded along the pier, cruised gently out into the estuary to view the sights, took a mystery coach ride from seafront to tea garden somewhere beyond the borough boundary – or spent almost all day and all savings in a pub or on a pub crawl.

From Pier Hill to Kursaal car park, along the Mile that was more half-mile, there were a dozen licensed wells from which to quench the thirst and celebrate the freedom of the moment. And since most coaches stopped en route, somewhere along the A127 or the A13, at some convenient hostelry or for passengers to attack the abundant supplies of bottled ale in crates stacked in the luggage compartment, the brewers and their shareholders had much for which to be grateful to Southend.

When the Londoners' Playground was so full during daytime and packed again after dark, after The Lights were switched on; when so many whirled and swirled in and around the Golden Mile that it seemed that the capital surely must be almost devoid of people; lots got deeply and hopelessly and blindly drunk. After closing time, in early afternoon, they would try to sleep it off in car park, on the beach, on seafront seat or shelter. After dark, they headed for a charabanc seat as welcome as port to a sailor six months at sea. But surprisingly, amid such drunkenness and in gatherings as enormous as the Wembley Stadium attendance on Cup Final day, there was comparatively little trouble. The world had not become anywhere near as generally and sweepingly violent as it would be long before the century was out; Southend was nowhere near as intimidating and provocative as it would become, much later. Of course there were fights, sometimes vicious and involving considerable numbers.

Of course there were occasional indecent and objectionable acts and threatening behaviour and petty theft. But in those busiest of all years, immediately either side of the war and long before the Mods and Rockers and Teddy Boys and the advent of mass car ownership, the potentially explosive situations in summertime Southend were mostly contained by just a few policemen. If the old black and white Westerns of one firm and fair, courageous, sharpshooting sheriff or marshal cleaning up a bad town and establishing law and order were more myth than fact, more Hollywood illusion that reality, so too was the retrospective review that had one or two big Bobbies controlling potentially unruly and drink-inflamed thousands.

Yet there often were only a few police officers between pier and Kursaal; and they did sometimes dish out summary justice to lawbreakers or troublemakers. They were able to rule largely by general consent: if someone asked for or caused trouble and was dealt with by a copper, the crowd were unlikely to intervene. They might at times even come to the aid of an outnumbered policeman under attack.

Tall and big and strong and imposing Bobbies were selected for duty along the summertime seafront, particularly that stretch where most visitors congregated as they flocked from coaches and trains. My own father, of the huge feet and hands, was among those who did duty here. I saw him on various occasions arresting or quietening or lecturing wrongdoers. He would give two warnings to miscreants to behave, to go about their day peacefully and without bothering others. He'd tell them once. Then he would invite them to look down at his size-thirteen boots and quietly insist that if they did not take heed, follow good advice and move along, they might well feel one of those boots several laceholes deep in a certain part of their anatomy. Most got the message second time, if not first.

Those who wished still to argue would suddenly and stunningly feel one massive hand grab them by a wrist, feel arm forced violently behind back and jammed upwards, before being spun then knocked to the ground. Next came the weight of two knees and one large policeman on lower back as wrists were cuffed together. Any particularly heavy, large or aggressive customer would be left in the prone position while the arresting officer – my dear old, funloving, soft-centred dad – summoned help with piercing blasts on whistle.

The less stroppy would be jerked unceremoniously to feet, then marched from the Mile to that quieter area behind the seafront buildings, alongside the Seaway car park, then accompanied through the backways to the Alexandra Street police station. Offenders who had caused trouble in Southend, particularly those who had shown violence towards a police officer, were before the court next morning. The local Justices of the Peace, the likes of the Heddles, from the family of strictly-religious Peculiar People and from an admired local business empire, dispensed speedy and tough sentences.

There was one particularly admired local copper who was not averse to settling matters right there on the spot, without having to trouble Your Worships. He was loved, in those days of which I talk. He was still much respected and regarded in the many years from when he retired around 1950 until he walked his final beat. His name was Gerard Sutton. Most local folk knew him as Gerry.

Big Gerry, not over-tall at six-feet among the many lanky giants of his era, was thickset, muscular, barrel-chested, fearless and frankly frightening when he wasn't smiling and joking. His bravery in the First World War had won him the Croix-de-Guerre, a rare and cherished award for a Tommy. When he returned to Civvy Street, when the Southend Borough Constabulary, formed in April 1914, was still in its infancy, he became Pc 31. In the twenties and the thirties, he was just the kind of man to keep an eye on summertime seafront.

Gerry became a legend. Trouble in a pub? Someone refusing to pay? Someone frightening staff and customers or starting fights? Gerry waded in, fists flying, few questions asked, quick answers supplied. On one memorable occasion he broke up a scuffle near the front entrance of the Kursaal. Then the main culprit, a big and intimidating, foul-mouthed man, rounded on Gerry. The copper was only hiding behind his uniform, goaded the man. He'd stay a mile away from trouble if he wasn't in uniform. It provoked some of the crowd to gather round Gerry and to take up the cries against him.

Gerry slowly took off his helmet and dropped it to the ground. Then he carefully and deliberately unbuttoned his to-the-neck tunic, eased it from his considerable frame and let it, too, slip behind him to the pavement. He looked, now, like some old bareknuckle fighter: which he was, really. His trouser braces stretched over an old-fashioned, collarless, button-fronted woollen vest with half sleeves that seemed moulded to Gerry's considerable frame. "I'm not hiding behind anything now, sonny," he said to the man who was spoiling for trouble. "Just make a move, son, then I'll sort you out."

It was shortlived and it was brutal. As the crowd moved back, forming a circle, the big man advanced on Gerry and swung a huge first. Gerry ducked, moved forward like a menacing tank and began slamming piston-like blows at his tormentor. As the man staggered under the onslaught, he was driven backwards to where he was forced suddenly to stop short, his retreat blocked by one of those great pillars that rose from the footwalk to hold the overhead canopy alongside the Kursaal entrance. Now, unable to escape, he was soundly thrashed.

He was saved when two more policemen burst through the crowd and each grabbed one of Gerry's arms and pulled him away. The man sagged to the ground. Gerry picked up his tunic, dusted it with one hand and put it back on. Then he replaced his helmet on his head and said, quietly, to the bleeding and bruised man slumped at the foot of the post, "You really must learn to behave yourself, sonny, otherwise you're going to land in serious trouble." The crowd broke into applause. There were no arrests, no charges.

When he retired, Gerry reckoned with a smile and a huge wink that he had received perhaps fifty black eyes while on duty. He never mentioned how many he may have bequeathed to others. He lived near the town centre, close to the then booming York Road Market and near the old Regal Theatre, main fire station and City Coaches depot of Tylers Avenue, which would disappear when much of central Southend was flattened and reshaped. His wife became wheelchair-bound and, summer and winter, often with open-necked shirt and sleeves rolled high on his thick and muscular arms, almost always with a smile and cheery words for passersby, Gerry would push her with apparent ease to the shops or for outings from home.

Long after he died, the legend of Gerry Sutton lived on.

THERE seemed, back then, to be so many unusual and outstanding characters around Southend: wellknown and respected coppers walking the beat or directing traffic or positioned in doorways, watching and waiting and comforting by their very presence; paper sellers, men and women, shouting the sensational news, offering the latest horse racing results, from their pitches, usually close to busy bus stops; bus conductors of familiar faces and familiar phrases; bookies' runners lurking in doorways and on street corners, waiting furtively to take bets in those pre-betting shop years when, so ludicrously and often so ineffectively, on-street betting was illegal; assistants in town centre shops who seemed to have been there, behind the counter, for ever; waitresses who returned every season to the seafront cafes, recognised immediately by sight, if not by name; waitresses in the High Street coffee bars and tearooms, who helped to give a familiar and cosy continuity and permanence to a town where we felt so at ease and at home.

If, as is likely, distance of time has lent enchantment to this picture of a Southend some six decades or so ago, one still may claim that we were more of a family back then. And as in any large family, there were memorable, harmless and unforgettable characters, most long gone, most still recalled.

7

DOWN our street back then, along the two sides of Burnaby Road, there were characters galore: enough to have peopled any Coronation Street-style soap opera of the kind that would arrive years later, long after we had reached the start of the Second War, survived it, then celebrated its end with a great street party.

There was Simon, for one. Well, us kids called him Simon, though not to his face, because we thought he was somewhat simple and even though there is that inexplicable, inherent cruelty about children, we never tormented him. His name was Clifford (you don't come across many Cliffords any more, among the newlyborn, do you?) and we thought he probably had a cog loose because almost every time anyone saw him, he was imitating a train, though he was old enough to know that this was not what boys growing big, usually did.

Simon – or Clifford – lived towards the end of the terrace on the southern side of the street, near to the great gasworks complex. His mother sent him at some time, most days, summer and winter, to the Goodings corner shop at the other end, for some item or other. He never walked, never ran: always adopted the same shuffling style with his feet, arms tight at side, bent at elbows, so that his forearms were at forty-five degree angle to body and he pumped them back and forwards as pistons on the wheels of a steam engine. He made loud chuff-chuff sounds and occasionally tooted, this human locomotive on a journey to the end of the road and back.

He went to some private or special school, which was definitely unusual for anyone from our street, and he moved away with his family while he was still young. The only news of him that filtered through, years later, was that he had gone on to become a Queen's Counsel – which just goes to show that boys who chug along minding their own business, might well be on the right lines for success.

An elderly couple nextdoor to the human engine and his parents, had one son, a Downs sufferer named Fred. In those unenlightened times, I don't think there was a school or special centre for Fred, so he stayed close to his mother and father, but joined us for some of our many street games after school, at weekends and in school holidays, ever smiling, always placid, rarely speaking.

The boys challenged each other to competitive marbles, a kind of version of lawn bowls, using little solid glass balls of differing colours and seemingly endless designs and patterns, played indoors on bare floor or carpet or outdoors on pavement or along the gutter. We mostly elected the gutter. A game began when a player clenched hands behind back, one holding a marble. Correct call by an opponent meant the player with the marble in hand must roll it first. He would usually send it a considerable distance along the gutter. When it came to rest, the next player would try accurately and at appropriate pace, to send his marble after the first one. A direct hit meant a marble had been won and would be collected. The game could and often did go on for ages, with several players each following the other, in turn, each missing the nearest marble ahead and constantly shouting, to remind opponents, "Mine's the Green Lady"... "I'm the Striped Ginger"... "The blue-dotted white's mine."

There were boys who claimed that their own very special marble had conquered countless others and had thus boosted their collections. They would challenge anyone to a game and considerable gatherings of lads would be attracted, in hope that the boastful might be exposed by some slick bowler of yet another marble of legendary achievement.

Much swopping and trading and offering – "I'll give you two Blue Streaks for your one Golden Globe" – and sometimes even buying and selling for cash, went on in the marble fraternity. Similarly, we dealt in cigarette cards, which were acquired first by parents who almost all were heavy smokers. Their loyalty to particular brands or temptation to try other makes, was sometimes tested by the type or variety of free cards given away in packs of ten cigarettes. I recall Wills, Churchman, Sarony and Ogdens among the brand names.

The cards featured coloured sketches of their subjects on one side, potted information or biography on the reverse. The likes of great footballers, famous cricketers, leading explorers and adventurers, stage and screen actors, great railway engines or species of butterflies made up the series. There was one set called Howlers. A trawl into my deepest memories reminds me of the kind of things they used to say: "Julius Caesar was a very strong man – he threw a bridge across the Rhine"... "The AD in 1066 means After Dark."

There were days when the cries would be heard along the street: "Anyone got a Tommy Lawton?"... "Who'll play me for a Flying Scot?"... "I dare you to go flicksy for a butterfly." Flicksy was a popular game with high stakes indeed. A bold owner of various cards would select one valued and sought-after card from his own collection and offer it for challenge. It would be stood on its narrow end, on the pavement, leaning against foot of wall, so that it was almost upright, a piece of coloured and printed glossy card, measuring about two inches by one inch. The challenger would stand or crouch some six feet away, then flick one of his own cards. If he hit and knocked over the standing card, covering it with his own, he collected it. If he missed, his card became the property of the other player.

Fortunes in cards were won and lost in our street and sometimes voices were raised and sometimes there were allegations of cheating and a bit of shoving and jostling and the very occasional scrap. Mostly, though, reputations grew: of the great and daring gambler who would risk any card against a flicksy; and of the deadshot flicker who rarely missed. If we had been the least bit smart, we would have completed our collections and kept them in pristine condition and sold them for fortunes when we were thirty or forty years old or even more ancient and wanted to settle down. But the next game or the next idea was always much more important and much more pressing than looking too far ahead. And we are all wise when it is too late, right?

We played a game known as Snobs or Five-Stones, too. The equipment, carried in the pocket in case one came across some hapless smartyboots with a penny to wager, consisted of five small pieces of baked and coloured clay, about the size of meat extract cubes. The skilled performer would group the five stones on the ground, then place left hand a few inches from them, fingers apart, arched and clawlike, fingertips touching ground. Then he would pick one of the stones, throw it in the air, and speedily and accurately tap the first of the remaining four through the first of the gaps between fingers before hurriedly catching in his palm the stone he had tossed upwards.

This excercise in concentration, timing and carefully-applied tapping of the stones between the fingers, in sequence, through one arch, then through the next and so on, was repeated until the player had four of the pieces beneath his left palm and the fifth safely in right hand. Now came the great finale. Left hand was moved, to expose the four closely-butting stones. The other piece was thrown upwards from right hand, which then scooped the four from the ground before being turned, palm upwards, so that the falling stone would join the other four.

Easy when one knows how, eh?

It was one of the many simple, time-consuming, attention-commanding, challenging and free pastimes of that other age, when even a private telephone around our way was as rare as the great sides of meat that hung in Mr. Cleverly's shining window, on hooks suspended from gleaming parallel rods of stainless steel. It was as simple, and yet in its way skilful, as the game of whip and top, which was looked on by us boys as a bit cissy, but played with much flair and devotion by the girls, who used sometimes to tuck their skirts or dresses into their tight, navy-blue knickers and do handstands up against the wall, looking upside down through their own outstretched arms at the passing, gawking boys.

The tops were wooden hand-me-downs: large toadstool-shaped toys that survived generations and thrived in the more depressed areas in the more depressing of times. The whips were homemade: long pieces of cane or stick with a dangling length of string attached to the end. The string was twirled round the stem of the top, which was released with a flick of the whip handle, so that it would spin along the ground, balanced on its narrow end, usually following the kerb line along the gutter, as the marbles in that other game. A player would chase his or her own top, ever so often flicking at it with the whip, so that it was propelled for great distances and for long periods of time before finally it came to rest, like some dizzy or demented ice skater suddenly halted after slipping out of control. Individual tops were ringed on their heads with differing colours of chalk, so that a magical, kaleidoscopic effect was created as the top followed its spinning way.

We played mixed roller hockey in winter in the parallel street, Beresford Road, with its houses along one side and the yawning summertime main car park of the Kursaal, where an estate would be built in the 1970s, on the other. Motorised traffic in these parts was unusual then: few private cars locally, just the regular tradesmen or passing vehicles to interrupt play. We took it in turns to stand watch at each end of the long playing area, one at the junction with Arnold Avenue and another where Burdett Road came into Beresford. Whistles were blown to warn the players immediately to leave the roadway and to stay on the pavement until the all-clear was sounded and the game resumed. Goal areas were chalked on the road surface, at each end of the pitch. An assortment of old hockey sticks, walking sticks held upside down and pieces of timber were used by the roller-skating players to whack the old tennis ball goalwards, to clear it from defence or to pass it to a teammate.

No one hurried home after a fall, for attention to skinned knee or grazed hand or elbow: the application of the then all-purpose iodine was more stingingly painful than simply waiting for any bleeding to stop and any hurt to lessen. Physical tiredness or boredom usually determined end of play. "I've had enough," one would say. "So have I," someone else would agree. It usually also signalled the need to assuage hunger or to be seated at home in time for Dick Barton's next adventure.

Sometimes Frank, a retarded, ever-smiling boy, would stroll into our territory from some neighbouring area. He would watch our roller hockey until the game broke up, then he would wander off to nearby alleyway to repeat a dangerous feat we had seen many times. He would go to about the middle point of the flank walls of neighbouring two-storey houses separated by narrow public right of way. Then he would push his back firmly against one wall and bend his legs at the knees, one at a time, pulling them back in turn to his chest, so he then could put the sole of one foot, then of the other, against the facing wall. Slowly, ever so slowly, without a word, he would edge his body upwards, first raising his back a few inches up the wall, then maintaining hold with one foot while moving the other yet higher, in rotation, until he gradually rose, walking up the walls, as it were, getting ever nearer to his eventual goal, the very highest level, where the front and back roofs met at a point along the centre of the building. One false move, one moment's loss of concentration, one split-second of panic and he would crash down between the sheer walls, to the metalled pathway below.

Ever amazed, terrified at the suspense, holding our breath, we would crowd each end of the alleyway, necks bent, watching the performance of a boy who, we did not then understand or realise, craved attention. He would rest momentarily at the peak of his tiring climb, then begin the descent, pressing a foot against the wall, slightly lowering his back, pressing the other foot, inching further downwards until he was once more on the ground. Then he would smile and wander away, perhaps not to be seen again for some weeks, when he would reappear and again perform the highly-dangerous stunt.

Frank's secret was safe with us, all of us. We felt that we might somehow be accused of encouraging him; that in being part of his occasional show, we were up to no good. So we kept quiet – as we did when we heard other things that did not make complete sense to us, but which we knew must be highly important and very, very serious, because the grown-ups who spoke to each other over their front garden walls when we were around, tried to whisper while looking shocked and serious. There was mention of some girl who was in some kind of trouble and she would have to pay a visit to a certain nearby chemist who could do things for girls with this sort of problem and nobody had better say anything out of place. And then there was that Mrs. So and So from just round the corner, who was at a funny time of life, whatever that meant.

We passed on this kind of information to the next of our acquaintance we happened upon, with a finger across the throat gesture and firm promises not to breathe a word to anyone else, on pain of death. We might not know what these secrets that became communal currency, actually meant, but there were lots of things that did not escape us, which we conveyed to others. And then one day old Mr. Mason stopped a crowd of us and gave us a public lecture.

Mr. Mason was very special. He had the MBE. There weren't many, if any, of these things down our way. The war was well advanced and we had come home from our two-year stay as evacuees among the funny-speaking people up in the Midlands and Mr. Mason had moved into our street in the meantime because he had been bombed out in London and he had been an important man in the docks before the war and he had been given a great honour to go with the medals he had gained in the previous war. So there.

He had a serious, lined face, with a wide moustache whose two ends had the appearance of cough candy twists, in colour and shape and gloss. I had tried on previous occasions to avoid him because he liked to stop to give advice and he always leaned forward so that his face was close to his listener's and his eyes pierced like needles. He was scary. We all knew him because in the summer holidays, his grandson came to visit and to stay and he joined our games and expeditions. On this particular day, when four or five of us boys were heading for the swings in the playground on the seafront, where they went and built the sealife centre a lifetime later, we could not escape the attention of Mr. Mason. He headed towards us, arms outstretched as though anxious to gather us together. "Ah, my lads," he boomed. "Just the boys I wished to have a little chat with." We huddled together, standing on the pavement, Mr. Mason leaning towards us.

"You're growing into young men," he observed. "Fine young men. I see that you stick together, which is a good thing. You must make the most of life and every opportunity. We are facing difficult times, still, although the war will soon be over. By the time it is, you will be well on the way to completing your education and thinking of making your way in the world. I want you to remember that good manners, courtesy and cleanliness are of great importance. Do you understand me?"

We all nodded, anxious not to prolong the lecture and to head for the Bucking Bronco, the Witch's Hat, the formidable Boat Swing and other free rides in the nearby playground. "That's good," he went on. "Now I want you to make sure that you stay out of mischief and do only good things and good deeds. None of you have been at it yet, have you?"

There was no response, because no one knew what on earth he was talking about and, in any case, it clearly was more accusation than question demanding answer. "Good," he beamed. "Good. Shows you're on the right path. That kind of thing comes later. Didn't try it myself until I was all of nineteen. You've a long way to go, yet. How it should be. Carry on, then, boys. Be good to yourselves and to each other and to your mums and dads."

He stood upright, edged the back of his right index finger along each end of his moustache, in turn, then strolled off. "He must be crazy," said one of our number. "Yeah, reckon so," said another.

We went off to the swings, never again mentioned this interlude and ever again managed to cross the street or dodge round a corner if we spotted Mr. Mason. When he died, some years later, after he had lost his wife, his empty house was one of a whole row demolished at the behest of Southend Council because someone thought it time to get rid of people and make way for something else. Forty years and more later, the empty space remains.

8

SO MANY people came to Southend in those long-ago summers, it was not unusual for the town to run out of bed spaces. There were plenty of hotels, but there were more than plenty of customers, too. The great and imposing Palace Hotel, overlooking a then often packed and booming pier, commanded a magnificent view – and commanded the more upmarket of visitor. So, too, did other fine buildings such as the West Cliff, the Westward Ho, the Overcliff, the Queens. These were the plush and posh and proud, multi-roomed hotels dating from the late-Victorian period, with their ballrooms and banqueting suites, their chandeliers and their uniformed staff.

There were many others in the borough, the Grand at Leigh and the Grand Pier, opposite the main entrance of the Palace, among them. There also were four in High Street: the Royal at its lower end; the London, at the corner of Tylers Avenue; the Middleton, alongside the exit from Central Station, where the hordes arrived on summer days and on those dark evenings when the illuminations attracted more families than any light might lure moths at night; and the Victoria, at the top end, where The Broadway met Southchurch Road.

Numerous smaller hotels in and around the town's central area and in many of the roads between the Westcliff seafront and the railway line, boosted the available spaces for staying guests to a huge total. Yet this still was not always sufficient to meet the demand. And, so, guest houses and boarding houses appeared with the certainty of hungry at a free feast, some a considerable distance from the seafront area. They were listed in the guide books and registered as recognised and welcoming places for short-stay or long-stay visitors.

But far more numerous, if far less formal or formally noted, were the private houses that offered bed and breakfast accommodation. Seekers of clean beds for the night and big meals to set them up for the day, flocked to Southend in my boyhood. Their demands for alternatives to the more expensive, more staid hotels were met by that simple, age-old law of economics: they were supplied by others. Homes in several streets within that great block of the town encompassed by Crowstone Road and Avenue in the west, Lifstan Way to the east, seafront at bottom and London Road-Southchurch Road at the top, became unofficial B & B establishments.

The most in-demand district was east of the town centre and out to Southend East Station, which had opened in 1931. Sometimes, in summer, the houses would advertise a simple message in a front window, in bold block capital letters on a white card: VACANCIES. Mostly, as the years passed and the trade substantially increased, the signs would rebuff those searching for somewhere to stay: NO VACANCIES.

My mother usually left a negative sign on display from Whitsun, as we then knew the late May bank holiday weekend, until well into autumn, when "the lights" were finally switched off and Southend turned from packed place to residents-only retreat. The two upstairs double rooms she let out to paying guests were rarely unoccupied, because our street was among the prime targets of the bed and breakfast brigade: close to the Kursaal, Golden Mile and seafront, a pleasant stroll away from the pier, a short tram – and, later, trolleybus – ride from the High Street.

There were homeowners in roads between High Street and Kursaal, seafront and Southchurch, who were said unofficially to employ barrow-pushing touts in the early 1930s. Many holiday-makers arrived without prior bookings for lodgings. They were accosted by out-of-work men willing and anxious to lead them to clean and inexpensive places, luggage conveyed on handcart, percentage of fee to be claimed after introduction of clients. But no such methods were necessary in our roads: there almost always were more seekers of accommodation than rooms available. Also, as the years passed, many holidaymakers returned year after year, for the same week or two weeks of the season, often leaving a deposit when they went home, against the fee for the next visit. They became as friends and relatives, although they paid for their lodgings and their food.

The idea of total strangers being welcomed into one's small and private home nowadays; of individuals or couples knocking on the door and asking for a night's or a week's accommodation, is somewhat hard to imagine. Yet, back then, there were few fears and few untoward incidents for those with spare rooms or sometimes even temporarily giving up their own rooms. There was just one occasion, in our home, when a problem arose with guests. My father resolved it with little difficulty and no argument. Two smartly-dressed and well-spoken men who had booked a room for a few nights, arrived after pub closing time on the first evening, much the worse for wear, staggering and noisy. They were invited to quieten down and to behave. They became louder and threatening. Dad grabbed first one, then the other, with a huge hand tightly on the elbow of each and shoved them out though the little front gateway and on to the pavement. "Wait there for your bags," he said. "Or else..." Then he strode upstairs, collected the men's as-yet unopened cases and deposited them heavily outside the front wall. "Get moving," he said. "You come back here and you'll forever regret it." The front door was locked and bolted, the lights switched-off. The men were never seen in our neighbourhood again.

They may well have slept on the beach. Plenty did, beneath the shore end of the many wooden jetties that poked out from the prom like so many different-sized fingers or in the shelters or, on the warmer nights, on the shingle, in the open. Such was the demand, so deep the human tide, it was rumoured that some people were so anxious or desperate to earn ready cash while opportunity was there, they sometimes spent nights in an amrchair while fee-paying strangers occupied their bed; and a few were reported to have camped-out in shed or under canvas in the back garden so that rooms were available to visitors. Such stories hardly raised eyebrows among our neighbours. After all, in the hard years ahead of war and in its immediate wake, there was much unemployment or, at best, seasonal labour. Many fishermen and boatmen lived in our community, proud people who worked hard when work was available and suffered quietly when work and income were scarce or non-existent.

We were relatively well-off and comfortable: my father had become a police constable in 1925, so he had a regular wage. He had three sons to raise and a mortgage to pay, while also always determined to save for a yearly holiday and for regular family outings. So my mother convinced him that in summer, the boys could share a room and guests could be welcomed – with their payments a decent boost to the income. He was reluctant, but eventually agreed. The downstairs front room became the guests' dining room, two separate tables set with starched, whiter-than-white laundered cloths and serviettes, the best china and cutlery brought from the sideboard.

A visitors' book was kept on that sideboard. The guests entered their details at some time during their stay: full name, in block capitals, signature, complete address, dates of arrival and departure. Almost all came from various parts of London. Many could look back at several of their own earlier entries, as the years in two decades sundered by war, seemed to flow like flotsam in a swift current. Mr. and Mrs. Strange signed-in more than any others: they first arrived, as strangers at the door, one August day in 1937. They returned the following summer and then again weeks before that awful September the following year, when the adults we suddenly saw and recognised as so uncharacteristically fearful and uncertain, wondered what the future might hold.

Then, after those years when everything changed and nothing would be the same again; when people went away, never to return; when families were wickedly robbed of sons; when houses were wrecked and lives were shattered; when children were evacuated to unknown and distant places and unknown and different people; when it seemed that the tears might never dry and the pain never ease; and when those seemingly lost, suddenly were found, the Stranges reappeared. They had survived the terrors and the torments of the years, the bombings and the killings; and Bill Strange had retired from his beat as a constable with the Metropolitan Police and he and his missus, a childless couple who had been born long before the 20th century, came back to Southend for a summer holiday. They sent a postcard, asked if they might book a room.

They came back like an old, much-loved refrain, picking-up where they had left off, as did so many thousands of trippers and holidaymakers from 1946 and onwards, as though nothing untoward had happened. Around nine in the mornings, after their substantial breakfast and their pots of tea, they went off. Mostly they did not return until nine in the evening, ruddy and glowing, smiling and tired, ready to sleep the long night. They had walked the seafront, strolled the pier, sat in their deckchairs, watched the passengers arrive and depart on the paddle steamers, gone into the Kursaal to watch the youngsters on the daring rides or to throw a few darts at prize targets, enjoyed their lunchtime pot of tea and maybe a plate of cockles or shrimps, listened to Happy Harry and others at the Speakers' Corner, then had their fish and chip supper, thoroughly at ease, contented, satisfied, appreciative.

One evening of each of the one or two weeks of every year that they came from Middlesex to Southend, to wonderful, invigorating, rejuvenating, reviving Southend, Bill Strange and his wife – always Mrs. Strange, to everyone; never anything else, as though she had no first name – went to watch the all-in wrestling at the Gliderdrome. They always took me, as their guest. It was absolutely fantastic for a boy just entering his teens.

There's a modern block of flats there now, on Eastern Esplanade, the first of the many similar developments beyond that open wasteland where once stood the great retort house, the towering and dominant Mr. Therm building and gasholders. The central, main entrance to these apartments used to be the opening to a little arcade of shops, to right and left of the covered walkway, with two floors of flats above. A man who created the most beautiful and intricate of glass ornaments with a blow torch and tiny pliers and infinite patience, sat in a tiny kiosk at the entranceway, often surrounded by admirers, sometimes selling an item to a customer. Tornado Smith, who lived in one of the upstairs flats, overlooking the seafront, often relaxed with newspapers or sunbathed on a balcony, though he was always in his familiar outfit and beret. At the far end of the arcade, away from the seafront, wide stone steps led down to the front of a large building that became a warehouse in later years for the Keddie department store of High Street and then, in time, was redeveloped with homes.

It was, then, when Bill and Mrs. Strange and so many more locals and visitors paid for admission, the Gliderdrome, a cavernous hall, with many-windowed sides to east and west. Most afternoons and evenings, roller skaters waltzed in ordered fashion to the music of a live band that sat on a raised platform against the building's rear wall. But on some evenings, Van Dutz, Clem Lawrence and the grapplers and grunters of the age arrived on the wrestling circuit and I was among the youngest to watch them perform – perform being the appropriate description.

It was theatrical stuff, even back then: beefy and muscular athletes, experienced in the many armlocks and holds, grabs and jabs, chops and throws, bouncing from the ropes, leaping and flying and crashing heavily to the canvas, all the while wagging warning fingers at opponent, muttering threats of reprisal, trying to outstare the man on the other side of the ring, as though the eyes might emit some laser beams. Mrs. Strange sat forward on her wooden seat, engrossed, controlled, silent. Bill relaxed, arms folded across substantial chest, smiling benevolently like a man at ease, grateful for the entertainment, enjoying the spectacle and the ring ridicule, appreciating the tricks and the physical strength of the combatants, yet knowing all the while that it was more show business than anything else.

But wise old Bill was very much in a minority. The great majority of those in the audience, mostly women, knew the goodie from the baddie the moment the first of the evening's four performing pairs entered the arena, climbed effortlessly between the ropes, disrobed, to display hairy chest or tattooed torso and to speak volumes merely through body language. Cynics claimed that the same two wrestlers, in reverse roles, would have met at some other venue on the circuit the previous evening; but this kind of thing didn't matter, anyway: it was the here and now that counted. And here, now, was a favourite and a rotter; and you could bet that at the end of the bout, right at the end, good would triumph over evil. Mr. Nasty would get his come-uppance.

Oh, how they screamed, these women packing the Gliderdrome. Normally quiet, peaceloving, law-abiding, even sedate wives and mothers, free for the evening from the home and working routine, were freed also from inhibitions: they went wild. They booed, jeered, hissed, shouted all kinds of threats at the baddies, some even approaching ringside to utter warnings and to shake fists before being gently guided back to seats by stewards. They urged the goodie to do all kinds of things to baddie, such as ripping arms out of sockets, breaking his arms, breaking his neck. The most-repeated urging was that Mr. Favourite should kick Mr. Nasty in the whatsits. Such entreaty was taken up as a chant by many women at many moments. It did not sound too nice to me, so I did not repeat it. Much later, one of our gang of local lads, Den, who was two years older, about fourteen going on twenty, and knew everything, explained in blunt terms what they meant.

Bill Strange was always still smiling when we strolled home in late evening, the excitement of it all still gripping me. "You must never take any of this seriously, son, y'know," he'd say. "They're strong and clever and brave chaps, these wrestlers, but it is all carefully rehearsed and worked out. They don't really hurt one another – but they are injured sometimes, by pure accident. It's all just entertainment."

Maybe. But another of the characters along our street, Jim Haswell, discovered the hard way that what goes on inside those ropes is not all play acting. We looked up to him, as youngsters, because he was six-feet and more, hefty, and a young man when we were boys. When he briefly joined the ranks of the all-in brigade, though, wearing long johns that had been stitched-up at the fly front and dyed a deep blue, he found himself mostly looking up at opponents, from his flat-on-the-back position on the ring floor.

Jim was thrown around quite a bit, so he speedily threw himself into a new career as a real actor rather than ring variety. He had lots of parts at lots of places and, come those early years of black and white television, he made regular appearances in the likes of Z-Cars and Softly Softly. Last I heard of him, he still lived in Southend and ran an entertainments agency. But that was long ago.

Even longer ago, Bill Strange and Mrs. Strange gave up coming for their annual holidays to Southend, as did other regulars to our home in summertime and to many other private homes. The VACANCIES signs stayed longer in windows; so long that they began to yellow and fade until, finally, they were removed. The older generation had grown too old any longer to travel to Southend for the kinds of holidays they had enjoyed for years and years. The younger people saw and cherished more distant horizons.

We never did know what became of Bill and Mrs Strange. They had been bit-part players in our story, yet important for all that. For a few summers ahead of the war and a few more after it, they had arrived with the regularity of Big Ben's chimes; but now their time had been and gone. They faded from the picture, as figures in a painting left far too long in bright light.

9

THE Stranges were not alone in giving up on Southend, the place they knew as a paradise to which they escaped for a couple of longed-for, saved-up-for weeks of those summers before and after the war. By coincidence, though not so surprising really, other regulars suddenly disappeared like bookies' runners when the police came into view. Maybe they had simply grown tired of doing the same old things, year after year. Perhaps age had wearied them to where they could no longer be bothered. Possibly, at last, they could afford better than bed and breakfast behind the Southend seafront and sought posher places or more distant destinations. Or, of course, some may have gone on that journey from which there is no return.

Whatever the reasons, in those early summers this side of the war, when everyday life remained often deeply grey and rationing was still in force, the familiar faces that had returned like welcome annuals in the garden, were no longer seen. Neither were these many old friends heard from. They had gone. And, so, the address book with the many repeat entries was closed, in the way the back cover shuts on a completed story. It was a story with loose ends, of course, for there would be no knowing what became of many of the characters who had left the set and not returned.

My mother knew that was it, then: the end for her of the summertime bed and breakfast business. Holidaymakers were still flocking to the town as though it were an oasis and they were desperate to cross the burning sand to reach it. But she did not wish any more to deal with total strangers. She put away the book and she put away the signs that had appeared in summer and she left it to others, in their own private homes, to offer food and lodging. In any case, a less demanding, safer, regular, once-a-week opportunity to earn pocket money in the tourist season came her way. She was courted as barmaid by the Plummer family, who ran the Foresters pub on the Golden Mile: a lovely, old-fashioned, extended family who knew Maud, as she knew them, from many years earlier.

The Plummers had taken Maud in, to work behind the scenes and, in time, occasionally to serve behind the bar, when she settled in Southend, a teenager with a baby son, a girl lost and alone and terrified, yet a survivor. A relationship with a handsome merchant seaman from America, when she was young and impressionable and living through hard times in the East End, near the docks, had left her in trouble when he sailed away. She went to stay briefly with an older married sister, at Folkestone in Kent, to give birth to the son, and then she came to Southend to take the job with the understanding and caring family at the seafront pub. She would in time meet the big policeman she would marry, who would unofficially adopt her son by claiming and naming him as his own and with whom she would have two more sons and live happily for more than half a century.

Older son Peter had served through the war in the Air Force and was now working at Croydon civil airport as a wireless operator before resuming his restless roaming that would lead to his finally putting down roots in American, marrying, raising a family and ending his days there. The other two boys were old enough to be left alone at home on Saturday evenings, listening avidly to programmes on the wonderful wireless, if Dad was on duty. So Maud accepted the Plummers' invitation: she returned after many years to the pub that had been her haven at the blackest time of her life, pulling pints to help to meet the apparently insatiable thirst of those who had "come to see the lights," but were determined that any touring and viewing of Southend's illuminations would be merely part of their few hours at the seaside.

It was a phenomenal time. In a clear and convincing challenge to Blackpool, with its famous illuminations, Southend's civic fathers in the mid-1930s had decided to light up the Londoners' Playground. The seafront, the pier and foreshore were transformed after dark into the kind of fairyland that most visitors had seen only in the new Technicolour in that booming age of cinema. It was a sparkling show shared and appreciated by us locals: great setpieces and multi-coloured lights along the length of the pier, magnificent displays from the Kursaal's glittering entrance along the Marine Parade and beyond, many-coloured and animated scenes on huge supports sunk into the mud a distance from the beach, so that the reflected glory was mirrored in the tide or on the glistening mud surface.

A charismatic character named Alex Hemsley White was the mayor. As a member of the Magic Circle, he certainly ruled over magical times for Southend. He was still prominent when the dark days of war were over; and when others had assumed the mayoralty, he was the dominant man at the top of the entertainment committee, the driving and encouraging figure at the helm when the roaring forties saw millions come to play or to stay and millions walked or rode the pier through what have been oft-recorded as the most successful of years for seaside Southend.

On Saturday nights in particular, in those early postwar summers, charabancs headed along the Arterial Road and the old London Road, like some ever-so-long strings of sausages, bound for the prairie-like car parks of Seaway, the Kursaal, Southchurch Park East. Excursion trains arrived at Central and Victoria Stations with the regularity of a metronome and the thousands who appeared from them, buzzed as bees following a leader to the Mile and the watering holes. Long before early-evening opening time, Maud and her colleagues and her friends and part-time employers filled pint glasses galore with the foaming nectar, lining them up along the bar tops, sometimes as many as three-hundred drinks, ready and waiting.

Then, when the doors were unlocked on the strict stroke of opening time, the customers flooded in like the onrushing tide, a great wave of thirsty funseekers, ready money in hand, anxious to grasp the first of what would be several pints of ale. From

LITTLE CHIEF JIMBO: Him paleface but heaps happy to pose for the camera in redskin outfit outside the front gate of the family home in Southend's Burnaby Road in the late 1930s.

MAGNETIC MONARCH: The ever-so-popular Royal Daffodil, one of the many pleasure steamers that attracted Jim and his boyhood pals to the pierhead in the resort's boom years (see Chapter 16).

SCRATCHING A LIVING: Sand artist Bill Robinson senior, who is discussed in Chapter 16, bends to his task alongside the near-end of the pier in this picture from the collection of the late Reg Sims, a prolific Southend amateur photographer.

CLASS OF '38 OR '39: Jim Worsdale, fourth from right second row from the front, and his contemporaries at Brewery Road School ahead of the war. Extreme right in back row is Les Still, who was later injured in an accident at Southend High and left Southend with his father, manager of the High Street Greys Inn Leather Store, and mother for a new life in New Zealand. Below: The author seated in the roadway, third from left in front row, at the Burnaby Road 1945 end-of-war street party.

SENTIMENTAL JOURNEY: Trams such as this one, pictured outside the Kursaal main entrance by the late Reg Sims in the 1920s, were still covering various routes in Southend during the childhood of this book's author. He often travelled from his home near the Kursaal to Warrior Square and High Street.

TRAIN OF THOUGHT: Steam engines such as this, pictured at Old Leigh, were familiar and regular sights until the Shoeburyness-Fenchurch Street line was electrified in the late 1950s. It was on one such train that Jim and his young friends made a daring, adventurous journey all the way from Southend East, out beyond the borough boundary to that distant place named Benfleet (see Chapter 14).

CLEAN FORGOTTEN? No, the many laundries of Southend past are still recalled by many older folk (see Chapter 1). They included the Ebenezer, one of whose vans is seen here, the Elton, Princes Street, Thorpe Bay and many others. The Albany is perhaps the best-known survivor of this time.

UNASSUMING GENIUS: Wireless pioneer and reluctant leader Eric Cole (centre) in 1951 at the 25th anniversary celebrations of the huge company that carried his name as EKCO. (See photo to the right and the Cole story, Chapter 13).

LOVELY MEMORIES: Girls such as 1949 Carnival Queen Barbara Murray, from Shoebury, and her court brought postwar glamour to Southend and to the then grand Odeon Theatre in particular (see Chapter 12)

WHAT'S THEIR LINE? It's the main assembly line at the Southend Ekco factory around 1950. Thousands worked for the internationally-famous organisation in its greatest years (see Chapter 13).

READING BETWEEN THE LINES: She was known as Madam Rene and in the hectic summer seasons of Southend past she read palms along the seafront. But the author of this book of reminiscences of Southend childhood looks back on half a century of newspaper life and comments: "I bet she could never have predicted how wonderfully life would turn out for me – even though plenty of others have told me my fortune!"

that astonishing moment to the again strictly-adhered-to call for last orders, the ringing of a ship's bell behind the main bar to sound 'Time, gentlemen, please' and then the closing of the doors on the final customer to depart, there was hardly a second to spare between filling glasses, refilling glasses, washing glasses, collecting glasses, taking the money to add to great cash mountains, giving change, exchanging banter.

In four hours, those who came to drink before perhaps going off to see the lights and those who had seen the light and quickly come to drink, would down a reservoir of beer. Remarkably, few tempers were frayed, few voices raised, violence comparatively rare, considering the circumstances and the Wembley-style crush of serious boozers. The beer flowed and then the customers ebbed away, doors and outside gates locked behind them.

The water tankers came along in the early hours to wash the streets of the Mile and in its vicinity – because when those mass hordes poured out of the pubs the night before, they had to pour out their liquid contents. Public conveniences were not always convenient and certainly not adequate for such demand. And, so, much water poured under the bridge – or, rather, under the jetty, in any available doorway, between parked coaches waiting to carry home all those who arrived in time for the return journey, and in or behind private gardens.

The alleyway between the houses in our street and those in the parallel road behind, was a convenient stop-off for desperate menfolk – and quite often women, too – mere yards from the Kursaal car park. At least, it was, if my father was not around to keep guard at its entrance, a huge figure deterring any attempts to pass his way or to pass the liquid intake.

When police duties had him elsewhere, there was no stopping those desperate or determined to sally into our alley and to water our back fences. There were times when this scribe, then into the teens, would lie in wait, behind high and stout fence and locked rear gate, several buckets and containers of fresh water ready for use. We had step ladders and a little chain of little humans to pass the buckets so that, once voices and other unmistakeable sounds were heard on the other side of the barrier, we indiscriminately tipped the water over the top, without a word. Screams, curses, spluttering noises and the occasional violent kick against fence greeted the sudden cold shower, but the dastardly deed usually worked as intended. Daybreak found other householders liberally washing the area immediately behind their own backyards with bucket after bucketful of carbolic-laced water.

Of course, we never let on to our parents that we had poured cold water on what others had considered a good idea. At this distance of time, I wonder still how we got away with it. But we did. We were survivors.

IT WASN'T only the war that we had survived. We had grown up in the thirties, when our homes were partly-heated in winter, with coal fires, and when our bedrooms sometimes were so cold that nightime frost embossed the insides of the window panes with thick and symmetrical patterns; and when forcing oneself to climb from warm bed on a freezing morning was a teeth chattering challenge, a considerable effort of willpower.

We survived without washing machines and tumble dryers; without refrigerators and television; without frozen foods and freezers; without central heating and takeaway eating other than fish and chips; without tea bags and visiting doctors with their Gladstone bags. For back then, before the official birth of the wonderful National Health Service that would become so over-used and so badly abused, we rarely visited a doctor and almost never called one, fearful of the fee and mindful of age-old, handed-down beliefs and remedies and claimed cure-alls. Take a spoonful of this or a spoonful of that. Wrap yourself in some itchy, padded, wool-like material known as thermogene. Pour down lots of cold water straight from the tap or pour on lots of iodine.

We heard about so many "gatherings" in our youth – gatherings of unpleasant, poisonous matter in boils and carbuncles and things as horrible in reality as their names sounded, because tight household budgets, followed by rationing and restrictions, often meant that some did not have the kind of diets that would become widespread and recommended and fashionable. The treatment was absolute torture: the application on the affected place of a hot poultice. This was a substance that was putty-like in appearance and consistency. It was mixed with boiling water, spread on thin linen, then applied immediately to the nasty place. The so-called cure was often far worse than the pain; so one favoured option was simply to leave well alone, to do nothing but allow nature to take its course.

Sir Alexander Fleming's revolutionary penicillin drug was still to be recognised and adopted until well into the war years. Antibiotics might well have been some foreign island, so distant was such a development in our time. Children with rickety legs walked the Southend foreshore mud, to strengthen their limbs and to savour and soak up the health-giving properties that were much heralded. Many of us swam regularly in the sea, totally unaware of something that would be known by later generations as environmental pollution. Us kids, down our way, ran into the sea, jumped from jetties into the sea, dived from breakwater and moored boats into the sea, took great mouthfuls of the sea and blew it skywards in our mimicry of whales.

We swam, parallel with the beach, from the loading pier to the big pier, then back again. Hadn't Princess Charlotte come here, way back in 1801, for the very purpose of sea bathing, as ordered by her physicians to benefit her health? Not that we were aware of such history and such patronage, as youngsters.

We were not aware of much at all, outside of our tiny part of Southend. As I have said, the borough was in effect a great grouping of hamlets and villages. We were self-contained, with our own butchers, bakers, grocers, chippies, newsagents, schools, Sunday schools, churches. Many menfolk even worked locally. In our neighbourhood there was the seasonal work of Kursaal and Golden Mile and regular employment at the great seafront gasworks, whose back entrance was at the far end of our street. Here, mountains of coal were added to with supplies brought by barge or coaster down the East Coast and into the Thames and to the iron pier that, since 1902, had straddled the Eastern Esplanade on great steel legs, perhaps only a hundred yards east of the then busy Corporation Pier. Great grab cranes reached down to unload the vessels and to lift the coal and then lower it into trucks that trundled high above the road into the works site. There, it was turned into gas that filled the holders that filled a considerable part of the local scene, and into various byproducts including the coke that fed home fires and boilers.

The gasworks hooter loudly announced the early start of each working day. It boomed confirmation of the midday break and the post-lunch resumption and it sounded again at day's end. It issued its mournful echo at the eleventh hour of the eleventh day of the eleventh month of every year for many years, too, to signal the two minutes' silence in memory of those who went off to war and never came back. We stood, then, in total silence, whether at school, work or in the home or in the street, as we stood in respectful hush when any funeral cortege came by and men removed their hats and bowed their heads. For all that we lacked, back then, we were rich in patience, tradition, manners, understanding and community spirit.

10

OUR community, as I have said, was similar to the many that made up the Southend borough: mostly self-contained and self-sufficient, so that we moved out of it only occasionally and briefly, for special reasons. One of these was when we had need or desire to visit the High Street. It was the heart of the town, the part to which all the main arteries led and where for years from long before my arrival, through my boyhood and teen years and much later, young and old, resident and visitor, made their way in pursuit of special purchases or simply to browse and gaze or to meet and eat or to visit the main cinemas.

I cannot recall from my young years seeing or hearing of any one empty shop in the High Street or in any of the streets that led off it, like limbs from a tall and straight tree. This was a busy and bustling, thronged and thriving, crowded and crushed, exciting and oh-so-alive centre which sucked-in people as might a whirlpool. It was versatile and vibrant, tempting and teeming, rousing and even regal, for its buildings survived in Victorian and Edwardian splendour through the first half of the 20th century and well after the war years until the Concrete Glass and Grey Age of the 1960s.

Back then, before the world shrank and the car and television changed our lives as never previously or since, we went at first by tram, later by trolley-bus and then by motor omnibus to the pulsating heart of the town. It was a place not only to look, choose, buy, but also to lift sagging spirits and to make even the loneliest feel suddenly part of a great mass of people united by the familiarity and the comfort and the lure of the surroundings. As I write this, without reference to any book or guide or listing, I mentally challenge the reader to stroll with me from the top of Pier Hill and up the eastern, righthand side of High Street to Victoria Corner – to the Vic Circus that was the hub of this grand town before it was so wickedly knocked around and reshaped much later – then across the road to Dixon's store and back along the western side of High Street to the Royal Hotel, at the corner of Royal Terrace.

More than half a century after the time to which I now hark back, I can recall most, although by no means all, the shops. Wandering now down Memory Lane, I see immediately to my right, opposite the Royal Hotel, the bow-fronted Royal Stores, a pub in my youth, and then the delightful Prospect House, which had become in my time the Going's store for anglers. Long before then, from the early 19th century, had lived there the town's first Medical Officer, Dr. Deeping, and there in 1877 was born his son Warwick, who became a novelist of considerable repute. His much-weathered gravestone is in the nearby St. John's churchyard.

I can recall when smoking was a widespread social pastime and acceptable; so a tiny tobacconist shop just beyond Prospect House, a branch of the Lewis chain, I think, was a busy place. A gleaming window allowed view of a considerable range of colourful cigarette packets and jars of various mixes of tobacco for rolling into tissue-thin papers.

Then, where the Tomassi family had its restaurant and ice cream parlour long before crossing to new premises on the opposite side of the street, was the Sam Isaacs fish restaurant. The father of a boy from our locality worked there, in the stark and bare basement, gutting and cleaning and filleting fish. It arrived from London's old Billingsgate in the early morning; and my pal's Dad was there to open the boxes and to begin to prepare the great volume of different cuts of different varieties ahead of the considerable demand from the customers upstairs that began with early lunches every day in the holiday and tripper season. We went just once to visit this man who spent much of his working life, from around five in the morning until perhaps one in the afternoon, a lonely figure in rubber apron and rubber boots, cutting and boning, scraping and cleaning fish. On that one occasion the smell was overpowering, the concrete floor wet and slippery. I could not know or understand, back then, why this poor man, when he escaped his daily grind, when he climbed those stairs from the semi-darkness back into the light of High Street, would head for the nearest pub and drink his fill in a race ahead of the clock and closing time.

As youngsters, we even thought it amusing that sometimes he would not make it all the way home, a walk down Pier Hill and along the Golden Mile and towards the gasworks, without stopping to rest on some garden wall and without, now and again, slipping behind such wall and into a deep sleep, where his wife might eventually find him. But, then, as a child, who can know how, why or what any individual may suffer, physically or mentally?

And what child can be aware that beautiful buildings and landmarks, historic links and great traditions, have already been swept aside in the cause of progress and that successive reminders of the past also are to disappear? How could any of us, in that time late in the war and just after it, realise that so much more was yet to vanish, including much of the High Street of that time?

Prospect House, the tobacconist, Sam Isaac's, restaurants, Martinelli the rock shop, a Barclays Bank branch in the greystone classic style, Maxie Lewis's law offices and other premises between the southeast corner of High Street and the corner of Heygate Avenue, survived for decades, if under different names and different uses, until that mass demolition and clearance for redevelopment of the area between High Street and parallel Church Road, bounded by Heygate to the north and the road at the south that runs now in front of the Royals car park.

Crossing Heygate, on our stroll along High Street, we arrived all those years ago at the corner shop of Dawson the chemist, with a dentists' surgery above. Then there was British Home Stores, followed by a string of small shops ahead of the corner of York Road. On the other corner, before Marks and Spencer extended and modernised, was, I think, a jeweller's, Hinds. We were about to reach the first of the many High Street premises and branches of the Garon empire, which began in small manner in the late 1800s and grew into an enormous, highly-successful, much-respected group that played dominant and prominent part in the Southend story.

Next-door – or, anyway, nearby in my mind's eye view – was the groundfloor cafeteria and upstairs restaurant of the Joe Lyon dynasty. And then there was the A. L. Edwards and Son store (the name can be seen to this day, on the building's facework above street level, although the business long since moved away and the groundfloor shopfront matches the ghastliness of much else in the vicinity). In this cool and sedate interior, behind polished wooden counters, gentlemen in pin-striped suits and with starched collars and cuffs to their pure-white shirts, served from selections of imported cigars and blends of tobacco whose aroma suggested a heady richness. Then, next to this, and ahead of the London Hotel that faced High Street and Tylers Avenue, was that most cherished of High Street stores, the County Jewellers of R. A. Jones.

Liverpudlian Robert Arthur Jones came South at the end of the 19th century and made his fortune as well as leaving clear evidence of his philanthropy in a town he came to love and which loved him so much that, when he died in 1925, thousands turned out for the funeral procession. He was buried in the grounds of his much-adored Prittlewell Priory, whose thirty or so acres of land he gave to the town for public use in 1920. Jones Memorial and Victory Sports Grounds were among other gifts from him to a Southend which was also served so well by his son, Edward Cecil Jones, a considerable charity worker and benefactor.

The richness of quality and variety in High Street (and, as yet, we have not ventured one step into any side street or offshoot) continued on the other side of Tylers Avenue. First, on the corner, was the Lipton grocery store, with its wonderful cheeses, bacons, provisions; its stone floor and marbled walls, suggesting great splendour; its white-aproned assistants, suggesting permanence and continuity when people with jobs stayed with them for many years.

And then came Offord's, or Offredi's, to use the original family name. There was some rare and exclusive air about this place. Bread, cakes, pastries, cheeses waited behind tall, glass display cases and counters for the passing customers to the front part of the shop. At the rear, behind double, glass-panelled doors, there was the main restaurant, where the town's great and good met at lunchtimes to discuss the state of business and of Southend, and where the wealthier sought reservations for high tea or evening dinner, served by waitresses in neat and crisp, black and white uniforms at tables covered in fresh, brilliantly white, starched tablecloths with matching linen serviettes and heavy silverware.

Among the long-surviving names beyond the Offord restaurant, along the short part of High Street to the railway bridge, was the J. R. Roberts department store, with its basement, ground and upper floors, and then two more Garon's outlets. One of these was the butchers where, in defiance of the much later generation's fears of dust and pollution and any possible passing plague or terror, great sides of meat and whole armies of turkeys, rabbits and poultry hung around, like the unemployed or the bored. It was a display of awesome quality and mouthwatering temptation; and visits late on a Christmas Eve might well be rewarded with a bargain when remaining produce was sold-off at reduced prices.

Beneath the bridge, where the roadway had long since been considerably lowered so that the railway track could be continued in the late 19th century from its then Southend terminus to Shoebury and its growing Garrison, was the Garon fish shop. The freshly-dead from the sea were laid out for inspection on great, gently sloping slabs, like mass victims in some giant mortuary; and live eels wriggled in huge, water-filled tanks, waiting for their own sudden and violent end.

We have strolled a mere halfway along only one side of High Street so far, yet the range of businesses is truly staggering. There are still small shops galore ahead. There is still to be reached, the noted drapery and haberdashery emporium of Sopers, where the new technology of the age sees assistants place bill and customer's cash in a little cylinder that is then screwed beneath a lid suspended from an overhead line that traverses the store like London Underground's Circle Line. A cord-pull sends a container on its journey to a central cash desk where, behind glass, a stern and obviously academic cashier and clerk carefully and patiently checks the contents, then sends the appropriate change whizzing back to counter, assistant and customer.

A few strides further, heading north, and we are at Warrior Square, where could be seen and boarded, until 1942, the final survivors of the various tram services that had originated in 1901. On this corner is Boots the chemist, a tall and impressive building as comforting and assured as a wise granddad. Upstairs, older folk enjoy afternoon tea dances.

Across the way, filling a substantial part of that final stretch of High Street before it ends at Vic Circus, is the Keddie department store. It was born in 1892 and, as we view it in 1942 or thereabouts, it is a wonderful, colonnaded copy of the famous London Selfridge store of 1935 and we cannot visualise that it will be rebuilt and redeveloped and extended in the 1960s, in the stark style of that decade. Even less can we imagine that, past its centenary, three years on, in 1995, when it would seem to be as permanent a fixture of Southend as the pier, it would die. It would suffer from a financial sickness that would attack far beyond the immediate Keddie family and the loyal staff who lost their jobs; it would be felt by countless customers and others, too.

To reach the Victoria Hotel, on the corner of High Street and Southchurch Road, we must pass yet another grand old grocery store, David Greig, amid the row of individual shops here. This is where they use great wooden paddles to pat the butter into blocks before it is weighed. It is where assistants in crisp and clean aprons cut succulent ham from the bone, sliced to the customer's own requested thickness, then laid carefully on the pan of the scales that are balanced with little brass weights. It is where, as youngsters, we are despatched, to wait to gauge when the bone itself, with its covering of meat now too sparse to be carved any more, may be ready for sale. To win the race to buy this prize takes skill and experience, as well as considerable patience, watching through the window for the exact moment to pounce and plead to purchase. This magnificent ham bone, now wrapped in greaseproof paper and carried home like some trophy claimed by a big-game hunter, will make the most delicious, inexpensive and filling of homemade pea and ham soup.

Our journey back down High Street, on the other side, begins outside yet another wonderful and extensive department store, Dixon's, on the northwest corner of the road and its meeting with London Road. Some forty years after they began to develop this side of the main shopping street, our parents still know it as The Broadway, even if officially it is High Street. Dixon's will be a landmark store for several decades until the family quits the rat race of retailing in the early 1970s. John Dixon will survive, in retirement at Thorpe Bay, until the late 1990s.

From this junction all the way down to the railway bridge, then to Cliff Town Road, beyond Weston Road and then Alexandra Road to the bottom end of High Street, this western side is as varied and as magnetic as the other side of the road. We note tailors such as Jennings and Rosenberg, jewellers, stationers, shoe shops, yet more evidence of the Garon influence with a baker's and, then, the same company's Masonic Hall and its cinema and restaurant.

There's a MacFisheries open-fronted, wetfish shop to compete with that of Garon's on the other side of the road, beneath the bridge, and then there is the majestic Odeon Theatre, which began life as the Astoria in 1935, built on the former Luker Brewery site in that golden age of the Hollywood cinema. Of all the dream factories in and around Southend; of all the settings from which to slip into a world of romance, adventure, escapism and even wartime propaganda, this is the mightiest of the mighty.

To the left of the Odeon, if one can take one's gaze away from such a splendidly impressive entrance and foyer, is a little shop with the most intriguing of front windows. This is Grays Inn Leather Stores. The whole window, right across the frontage from the left to the narrow entranceway at the right, is concave. It gives the impression of – well, not being there at all. Many a time, we look at the displays of goods, at the purses and bags and wallets and leather-bound items, and then we reach forward, sure we can actually touch them, until forehead or hand collides with glass.

Mr. Still is the manager here, as we get to the end of the war and move towards peace. I know, because his son Leslie is in my class at Southend High and there is a brief time when he and I and a boy named Alan Gibbs, whose parents have a baker's shop in Southchurch, form a musical trio to play at the St. Erkenwald's youth club. Les has piano accordion, Alan nicely tinkles the ivories and I try to keep time in my amateurish way on the drums I have gradually bought from secondhand shops and put together as a kit.

Our attempts at entertaining and being spotted by a talent scout from the West End or Hollywood, do not continue for long. There is a sudden, shocking and tragic interruption. Les is looking one day into his desk when he should be paying attention to the teacher, and he has the lid raised so that he is hidden behind it. The form master, a nice man, casually lofts a book from front of class, intending that it should strike the lid. But at that very moment, by wicked and seemingly impossible odds, Les lowers the desktop and the book hits him in the eye and in time we learn to our great horror and sadness that this one tiny incident has cost him the sight of that eye.

There is legal action and when it is over and done, Les and his mum and dad leave their home in Heygate Avenue and go off to make a new life in New Zealand and we never see or hear of them again. The Grays Inn Leather Store disappears, too, in time. So does another of its near-neighbours, the Middleton Hotel, which is on the corner of another chunk of High Street which also will vanish, the wide roadway leading to the northern side of Central Station. Garons have more shops along this part, then we reach Cliff Town Road, with the wonderful Rossi milk bar on its lower corner and, opposite, at an angle from the road, Railway Approach, leading to the main entrance of the station, lined on its righthand side by little offices of the town's many coal merchants. (There are more, similar, offices close to Victoria and Southend East stations, because this is when coal still warms our homes, stokes our steam trains and turns the wheels of industry).

From Cliff Town Road to Weston Road and then to Clarence Street, we pass a string of shops including a printer and stationer named Francis, a florist's, jewellers, tailor's, a bank, the substantial store of Owen Wallis, ironmongers. Close to this, on the corner of Clarence Street, we can gaze into the windows of James the baker and drool over the cakes and pies and tarts and iced wonders freshly prepared mere yards away, at the bakery in the side street. And then there's more: a Millett's store with little canvas tents rigged-up for display along with the cooking stoves, pots, pans, waterproof wear and the assorted paraphernalia for those who would sit in the open all night and fish or take to the woods and hills, where a multi-bladed knife is as necessary as two Boy Scouts to rub together to spark a fire in damp wood in the dew-laden dawn.

Now we approach another branch of the Rossi ice cream and milkbar family concern, a coffee house whose narrow front hides the depth of its interior and the depth of its appeal to young folk. The Woolworth store is next door, with its bare wooden floors, its aisles between great, wide counters tended by uniformed assistants and its upstairs for yet more display. And next to this, on the corner of Alexandra Street, is the pub we known as the Bottom Alex (the Top Alex being at the other end of the street). Across the road, where High Street yet continues for its final stretch, a fish and chippy outlet is run in this age by a family, one of whom has a nice house near the bowling green years later and falls foul of some of the planning officers when he does some improvements of which they do not approve.

The saga continues for a while, so that the man decides to make known his views of the bureaucrats by naming his house Llamedos. Some thought it was Welsh, but in time word spreads through the town that if you spelt it backwards, the message would become clear. Our window-gazing, shops-noting stroll up one side of High Street and back down the other, is nearing its end; but there are yet establishments of considerable note. We have reached the double-shop of Birn of Southend, complete men's outfitters and tailors, ski and riding specialists, stockists of ladies' swimwear. It is the province of Bobby and Joyce Birn, both of whom in their own ways will serve the town so unstintingly, she as a Justice of the Peace and great supporter of her husband, the man who creates and nurtures the Southend Music Club and turns it into perhaps the biggest of its kind in Europe. Time will come, in 1991, some four decades after this moment, when Bobby, who already holds the MBE, will become the twenty-seventh recipient of the honour of Freedom of the Borough, with more still to follow him before the millennium is done and then into the next one.

The Music Club is a wonderfully successful and admired organisation; the cultural balance against the cockles and Cockneys side of this town of dual personality or even split personality. From these early years after the war, through the decades and into the 1980s, Bobby Birn will, through his contacts, his charisma and his enthusiasm – and at no little personal expense – bring to Southend the world's finest musicians, singers, orchestras for sellout concerts for a club with a thousand members and a waiting list. This club would die after Bobby, but at the time of our High Street tour, it is in its lusty childhood and growing bigger and stronger.

At this time, too, the acclaimed Cotgrove fish restaurants are seemingly immovable anchors in High Street, even if planned redevelopment forces the family ship to drag anchor from one side of the road to the other and even though, at a time we cannot foresee, as this 20th century is a tad beyond its halfway stage, the family will give up business in the stormy seas of change. The Cotgroves, from a famous Leigh background, will commit themselves to years of business and civic involvement before calling it a day.

Below them in High Street, next to the Royal Hotel, yet ahead of them in opening a town centre business, is the great and impressive, Victorian store of Brightwell, draper, milliner, haberdasher, hosier. It had begun what would be an 80-year life, or thereabouts, late in the 19th century, the child of John Rumbelow Brightwell, who would become a Justice of the Peace and also serve twice as the town's mayor. In our time, you see; in this golden age that began for Southend's trading heart towards the nightfall of the 1800s, continued through the dawn of the new century and well beyond its fifty years, the town is served by so many family-owned, family-run businesses whose involvement embraces civic and social responsibility.

These are dedicated, devoted, determined individuals. The High Street is theirs to share, to shape and to shine, and never, even in a nightmare, would they foresee what would become of what they left. Never for one awful moment could they have imagined that High Streets in so many towns, not only in Southend, would become low streets in the shadow of the car and access to parts never previously reached.

11

BUT it wasn't only the High Street that was such a fascinating, motivating, stimulating, intoxicating, pulsating, exhilarating feature of Southend through my boyhood years and beyond. No, back then the town had a big heart that fed and served the limbs attached to the main shopping thoroughfare. The biggest of these was at Vic Circus. It can only be imagined now, behind closed eyes and in the deep recesses of the mind, by those who actually knew it before the brutal surgery that removed many parts of the whole, oblivious to the pain caused and the suffering that would linger on and on.

    The Vic Circus and the High Street and the town centre shopping streets that I wandered, as a boy, were parts of one complete, big, thriving, healthy body. Some knew the Circus as Vic Corner. Older folk referred to it still as Cobweb Corner, after the pattern formed by the overhead power lines for the trams, where the routes arrived from several directions and converged at this great turning point. Whatever the name, the large slice of the town that would be excised a couple of decades on from this time we now review, was famous far beyond Southend. Trains had arrived since the end of the 19th century at the station here, the second to serve the town. Still, in the great yard to the south of the station, buses came and went to many towns and villages across southeast Essex, all of which looked to Southend as the place for entertainment, shopping, working and relaxing.

    With Basildon still to be born as a London overspill New Town in 1949 and with Rochford, Benfleet, Canvey, Rayleigh, Wickford, Pitsea, Laindon merely rural neighbours, thinly populated and criss-crossed by unmade tracks, Southend had no serious competition: it was mighty and majestic and usually packed with people. Those who did not arrive at the Central Station, mostly arrived at Vic Circus, on trains or on the buses that served Foulness, Wakering, Paglesham, Canewdon, Rochford, Hockley, places that in our youth, ahead of mass car ownership, were as remote as the Shetlands. Other buses came and went from just west of the Circus, in London Road, with their destination signs indicating Hadleigh, Benfleet, Rayleigh, Grays.

Smokers travelled on the upper deck, where on wet and cold days the inside windows ran with condensation and the fug hung like a thick and dank blanket. When all seats upstairs and down were taken, the conductor would allow on sufficient standing-only passengers to fill the lower centre aisle, each clinging desperately to anything immovable in an effort to remain upright rather than fall into some unsuspecting, seated stranger's lap.

The busy and bustling Vic Corner hub, which would by the late sixties and early seventies be bypassed and underpassed and generally knocked about like an aged prizefighter meeting his doom at the fists of a giant young challenger, had four spokes in its wheel: Victoria Avenue from the north, High Street to the south; London Road to the west, Southchurch Road to the east. There were public toilets beneath an island in the centre of this great junction: an island in a sea of bus and motor traffic, so that reaching it was the prize for dicing with disaster or even death.

On weekdays, Saturdays, Sundays, bank holidays, sunny days, scorching days, freezing days and thoroughly soaking rainy days, policemen here stood on point duty, white gloves and white armlets over dark tunics helping to make clear the signals to drivers. Traffic at the busy, four-way junction was kept on the move, each of the roads given its priority turn while the drivers in the others waited with a patience that would disappear like manners, courtesy and understanding by the time the Swinging Sixties had swung the pedulum far away from what many of the earlier age knew and understood. And what brought so many of these locals and outsiders to the town, before they even wandered the High Street and the many other shopping streets, was The Talza.

Well, it wasn't The Talza, strictly speaking: it was the Victoria Arcade, a 1925 version of indoor shopping mall, of which the Talza was merely a part. Ah, such nostalgic thoughts are prompted from childhood by recollections of sorties into the dark walkways of this wonderland, which was marked to its south by Southchurch Road, to its north by a long-since-erased Broadway Market, a road roughly where the ring road of this age passes beneath those great and ugly, splayed concrete legs that carry the overhead footpath from Victoria Station to the Victoria Plaza, Hammerson precinct as was. To the west, the arcade was fronted by shops where, now, the plaza faces the multi-screen Odeon; and to the east was the length of Milton Street that would become the road of today between Southchurch Road and the ring road.

Inside this great square of an area that was formed by the many shops and the few little houses along its sides, the arcade was as busy and buzzing as a hive. It was perfumed by the smells of bacon and biscuits, fish and fowl, and underfoot sawdust; it was alive to the sounds of voices, the chink of china in a shop were plates and saucers and cups and dishes were stacked high, and the assorted barks, miaows, screeches and whistles from the pet shop.

There was a Bobin bookshop with its own exclusive aroma of paper and print. There was a hobbies shop, its window packed with boxed model planes, Meccano pieces, Hornby train sets and much, much more, so that it was a marvellous place of displayed and hidden treasures. There was an open-fronted store ringed with big, glass-topped tins of biscuits such as Iced Gems and Garribaldis and broken pieces. And there was a surgical goods place where no one wished to be seen to linger and to look for too long, for some mysterious reasons. Its window display rarely changed, yet remained so fascinating. There were bowls and dishes and straps and belts and pipes and pads and trusses and probably packets of three for the weekend, sir, that otherwise were purchased by grown-up men from the barber once they had been short back and sided. As the broadsheet News of the World used to proclaim back then, when we read it away from our parents' gaze, shocked and stimulated by cases of naughty vicars and nabbers of clothesline knickers, all human life is here. The arcade was as fascinating and captivating as any Eastern bazaar – and possible even more bizarre. Outside it, on its fringes or nearby, the Blue Bird Cafe was considered a bit – you know, daring, because it stayed open late when everywhere was closed and the police regularly looked-in on the villains, narks or rascals often to be found hunched over the tables, behind the steam-clouded windows.

A classmate of mine at the High School, name of Hammond, lived in a little cottage that backed into the arcade and faced Broadway Market, its front door immediately into its front room, which opened on to the pavement. Attached to it, in the terrace, was a tiny shop in which his father sat for hours mending boots and shoes.

A Mr. Heath – not the one who didn't get along with a Mrs. Thatcher a lifetime later than the period of this essay – had a large and eye-catching bicycle store where the Hercules and Raleighs; the sit-up-and-begs and the ones with handlebars like drooping moustaches, stood or hung from rails in the window. Back round the corner, coming out of Broadway Market and turning left towards the Circus, there were a few little shops above which was the bus crews' canteen, then came Garon's Corner, bending round from the end of Victoria Avenue and into Southchurch Road, with a cake shop, tea rooms, greengrocery. Standing above, as though on guard duty, was a tall clock tower with faces looking towards where the shoppers and workers of this more leisurely age, had the time to glance up to check the time. When its own time was up, the demolition day nigh, time was called on much that many knew and loved through its cosy familiarity.

When the bulldozers ploughed into Southchurch Road, they unceremoniously smashed down the places that stretched eastwards from Garon's corner to the junction with the western end of Warrior Square, wiping out names with the ease of light pencil marking dismissed by an eraser. The New Vic cinema, where the first of the daring Continental films had played in Southend to choosy audiences, a place also at some time known as the Civic News Theatre because it featured newsreels and magazine programmes, disappeared. So did the Thomas drapery and household linens store, a sedate and orderly place where time was devoted to customers and old-fashioned standards were maintained. Its Dan Thomas had gone off in wartime to serve his country and to become an unassuming, modest hero who suffered the most awful of wounds. Dan had played considerable part in fighting-off the enemy, but the progress of the town of Southend was too much for him. One wonders what might have been his thoughts in the years until his death in the late 1990s, when he saw the town centre of that time.

The tasteful Gilbert music store, with its fine window displays of grand pianos, also found that the tune was called by the council in that sweeping decade of smash and bash and replace. Yards away, another old favourite, the St. Ann's Manufacturing Company, also surrendered its characterful offices and main town centre works to the destroyers. William Sharpe had started the firm, towards the end ot the 19th century, with a little shop just round the corner and a horse and cart for deliveries. He advertised as a builders' merchant and decorator, with oil paints, lead and glass for sale. Fortunately, more than a century later, the company remains a family-run concern, based in Leigh and with main offices, works and depot off Sutton Road, opposite Jones Memorial Ground. As this was written, St. Ann's was among the few long-lasting businesses that survived the massive changes and still survive. Rossi, Tomassi, Raven and Haven are others.

Further east in Southchurch Road, the London Co-operative Society had considerable presence immediately after the war and onwards, as it did in many parts of the borough. It paid its little dividends to its member-customers until its own number was up.

Retracing one's steps, back to the Circus and crossing into London Road, the view to the immediate right, just beyond where the tree-lined Victoria Avenue stretched like the grand drive to some stately home, was inspiring: a most pleasingly-designed, red brick and stone building that had been opened by the Countess of Warwick in 1902 to great public acclaim and to meet the town's growing need for school places. The Municipal College or Tech, as locals knew it for more than sixty years, would be another victim of the slaughtering of the sixties, making way for a car park and open space until, almost three decades later, a multi-screen Odeon complex would rise.

Other long-standing buildings and long-lasting and familiar names would go, when this author himself had temporarily left Southend on journalistic jaunts and assorted duties; too many now to note. Among those to disappear were the many grocery shops of the Schofield and Martin's Stores chain. Albert Martin, like many other businessmen in the earlier years of Southend as an incorporated borough and later county borough, did not only serve his customers; he served the town in a civic sense, too. By his death in 1943 he had been some forty-seven years a councillor and twice the mayor. His familiar and friendly and amazingly-stocked shops lived on long after. The first, I think, had been in Alexandra Street, to the right of the building opposite the Rivoli cinema of my youth, the home of the County Borough Treasurer. I personally recall others on Thorpe Bay seafront at the corner of Plas Newydd and in Leigh Broadway.

Martin had sold out, long before his end, to a Mr Waite and a Mr. Rose, whose names were joined as the Waitrose chain of the John Lewis empire and, thus, are still in a sense with us in Southend. Very much still in the town are Ravens, prominent in Cliff Town Road although in this commentator's boyhood and until well after the war, the family firm was based in London Road, just west of the Circus and near to the then Trinity Church, in a building which, even in the new millennium, remains clearly recognisable, above the groundfloor of its present occupants, a building society, as from the 1930s.

Raven and the handful of names that spanned the 20th century, with Haven of Hamlet Court Road approaching its own century, are as welcome to older Southenders as home after a long time away or a familiar face in a crowd of strangers or a signpost when one is hopelessly lost and alone. There was a cosy continuity about Southend for so many decades: names that were known and trusted, buildings that were somehow friendly compared with the faceless that would follow.

The changes to the town and in the countless characters who have been part of so wide-ranging and remarkable a story, have been truly astonishing since the 20th century moved into its second half. The personal view expressed here is that, overwhelmingly, looking back with that wonderful asset of hindsight, the balance of benefit is far outweighed by the heaviness of loss.

12

WHEN we weren't at work or school or browsing around the High Street and the bustling York Road Market and the Victoria Arcade; when we weren't busy doing any of the many simple things that filled our young days, we went to the pictures, or to The Flicks, as some said. The 1930s and that slice of the 1940s from the end of the war was a golden age for the cinema; and it was just when we were of an age to be wakening to its mass influence.

Suddenly, in those black and white images, we were transported far beyond our own little part of the borough and far even beyond the borough boundaries into the wide and weird and worrying and wonderful world. And, sometimes, even into the colourful world thanks to that most marvellous of new inventions which added hues and tints and shades to films such as the Wizard of Oz and Robin Hood.

Fact and fiction, funny and frightening, ridiculous and realistic – the world on Celluloid came to visit us, here in Southend, at a time when private telephones were for the select few, uniformed telegram boys still pedalled the streets to deliver urgent messages and await replies, and motorcars suffered punctures to their tyres as regularly as the ego of the pompous would be deflated when television discovered satire decades later.

All of a sudden, through the silver screen, we became spectators of the spectacular; of deep and tender romance, of thwarted passions, of the impossible becoming the possible. We had heroes to admire and even to worship; villains who would, we knew for sure, get their come-uppance in the end, because that's the way it was. Right was right, even when it sometimes tested us by seeming perhaps so wrong, and right was might and would triumph.

Grable and Grant, Bogie and Bacall, Fontaine and Flynn, Cagney and Cooper, Rooney and Robinson – individually, these and so many stars filled the screens with their personality and their publicity and filled the seats. And in and around Southend, these seats totalled in their thousands. Anyone able and willing to go to the pictures every night of a seven-day week could do so without returning to any one cinema – and still not come anywhere near visiting all the picture houses.

I do not recall visiting the Kursaal cinema, the nearest to our home, but my late parents reminded me long ago that I went with them to this tempting place, alongside Southchurch Avenue, in the main building of the then great complex, mostly for afternoon matinees before my school years and when my father had finished a shift as a policeman or ahead of a night duty. It had opened soon after the birth of the 20th century and survived until the late 1930s, by when it had serious competition and in any case was needed as a site for one of the many different attractions in the fascinating amusements complex.

I did not get to the Hippodrome in Southchurch Road, near Victoria Circus, when it was still under that name, because it dated from way back in 1909, when it had opened as a live theatre with some 1,700 seats. But as youngsters we came to know the upper balcony which was popularly referred to as The Gods, for we often queued to sit in this high and steeply-sloped section when the pleasure palace that had featured the country's greatest artists of Music Hall, had become the Gaumont Palace moving picture theatre. It survived under that title until early postwar, when it turned into simply the Gaumont, beneath the Rank umbrella, until it was smashed down in the mid-fifties to make way for a supermarket.

There was yet another cinema immediately to the rear of the Gaumont, the Strand from the 1920s that became the Essoldo for the last few years of its life, in the fifties. It had two entrances. One was at the end of a tiled-like-a-public-convenience, covered alleyway, a kind of long, Underground-type tunnel that poked through the High Street shops on the eastern side to a narrow, parallel lane where were the cinema's doors. The other entrance with paybox was behind the stage and screen, in Warrior Square. Oh, what joy was a Friday evening visit to the Strand. Sometimes we arrived early to make sure of a seat for Amateur Talent Night. Singers, tap dancers, jugglers, impressionists, comics, conjurers and contortionists took their turns on the dusty, bare wooden stage, between second film and main feature. They competed against one another for the loudest applause that would win them some small prize – and competed against the wicked and naughty audience, most of whom had come to enjoy the films and to exchange banter or give the performers hell.

I hold one particularly vivid memory, of a young lad in sailor's uniform, who sang Anchors Aweigh, accompanied by a pianist. He was clearly as nervous as a best man cajoled for the first and last time into making a speech at a posh wedding. His voice was breaking and off-key. And when the most cruel customer in the house yelled "Get 'im orf" and a slow handclap began, he burst into tears and hurried out of view. The Master of Ceremonies instantly appeared, in a blacktie outfit whose jacket shone like worn, polished leather and whose trouser knees suggested he had knelt in silent prayer on the dusty floor before hostilities commenced. "Now then, ladies and gentlemen," he bellowed. "Let's be fair. This is amateur night. Give everyone a fair hearing."

"B----- off," was the response from a stentorian voice in a call that was echoed by others. Attendants appeared, their torchbeams flickering like fireflies in a black night, walking the aisles and urging patrons to behave themselves. Above the din, the MC endeavoured to announce the next act. We had no idea what he had said, until a singer in a pretty dress, twirling a parasol, stepped daintily into view, to piercing and shrill whistles. This Friday night was no different from any other Amateur Talent Night. No winner, far as one can establish, ever went on to any great heights from an appearance at the Strand – unless, of course, it was to a seat in The

Gods at the nearby Gaumont, to watch a film. The height there was dizzying.

But Amateur Nights were not the only diversions at the Strand to make it different, very different, from its many competitors, most of them smarter and bigger and more modern. No, there were special Fridays when the cinema was packed because of Hocus-Pocus Night. I say, I say, I say. Funny things happened on the way to the Strand theatre on these nights. Yes, indeed. Mostly mature women comprised the audience. And mostly they each had a carrier bag or holdall. Well, they never knew what they might be called on to produce, you see.

The Master of Ceremonies from Amateur Talent Night was on duty for this hocus-pocus nonsense, too. He'd stand before a microphone as tall as a large sunflower, its shout-into-here head as big as a prize bloom, and yell such commands as, "First one with two clothes pegs wins a prize." Women would scamper down the gently sloping aisles, jockeying for the lead, all the while scrabbling with hand in their magic bag in search of the necessary items that might just win them a half-crown or two free tickets for a film show the following week. They'd push and shove, pressed against front of the stage, shrieking as the audience shouted and clapped and stamped, waving in desperate hope of attracting the attention of the man at the mike.

One naughty night the MC declared with unusual daring that provoked great bellows of delight and raucous laughter, "First one up here with two pairs of knickers wins a surprise prize." Then, as the rush towards the front of house began, he added, "'Course, I don't mean wearing 'em – I mean 'aving them about their person, if you follow." A huge woman won the five shillings the MC pulled from his pocket. She had plucked from a carrier bag two enormous pairs of near-white drawers that seemed big enough to rig a sailboat.

The next call was for a full set of hair curlers. The first woman to reach the front was snatching a thin scarf from her head as she hurried forward, to reveal her own hair still tightly held in rows of curlers. Around about that time there was a poster campaign for a brand of shampoo that proclaimed 'Friday night is Amami night.' For this woman it was Amami and hocus-pocus. The fullhouse crowd laughed so loudly and applauded so vigorously, it must have been funny.

But by 1960, at the dawn of that decade that wreaked such change and havoc in Southend, the laughter had faded, the old entertainment seen as old hat and redundant. The Strand of my youth, which had long since become the Essoldo, echoed only to the sound of crashes, bangs and wallops as the building was extensively altered to create the town's first supermarket, facing Warrior Square, a baby of the entrepreneurial David Keddie, who would later extend his department store and swallow the supermarket in the process. By the mid-1990s, with the Keddie family's town centre business more than a century old, it collapsed and died under a sea of sadness and recrimination and rumour occasioned by squabbles over financing.

Only a few years after the Strand-turned-Essoldo closed for a final time, so did Garon's cinema in High Street. The boom years of cinema, that were not to return until a new generation spawned multi-screen complexes and films that left little to the imagination, were over. The dreams that had fed my youth and carried us through the war years, through the forties and into the fifties, were ended.

But the memories, so many memories, linger. Garon's, opposite the Keddie store, next to the family firm's Masonic Hall and other High Street premises, now the site of a totally-different row of shops, offered its six-hundred seats at ninepence each, sit anywhere you choose, when I was a regular visitor. A woman played the organ at some time during my period of patronage – and before and between films, water fountains played at either side of the screen, illuminated by multi-coloured lights. One of the boys in our street used to say that the organist was "one of the Bagas." I always misheard what he said. Years later I learned her name and of her considerable reputation in the world of music – Ena Baga, youngest of four musically talented daughters of composer Constantine Baga.

The family had moved to Southend from London around the First World War because Ena suffered from chest problems and a doctor advised that she should be near the sea. They lived in one of the terrace of tall houses towards the top of Southchurch Avenue, then known as Brewery Road, just ahead of what became the junction with Ambleside Drive. Ena went to the Sacred Heart School, a short distance away, and soon became a local church organist.

She went on to play the piano for silent films at Garon's Bioscope. It had opened in 1911 and was much extended in 1929, after the arrival of talkies and the end of the need of live accompaniment to paint the musical pictures of delight and despair, happiness and horror, danger and daring, romance and roguery. Years later Ena briefly returned to entertain at the organ.

We had grand value for our money, even though the price of seats had risen to one shilling, all parts. We watched trailers for the next week's attractions, cartoons, newsreels, a second feature and a main film. And there was the selection by the organist, fountains twinkling, so that a visit to the cinema lasted at least three hours.

Ena Baga was still alive and still occasionally playing organ when last heard of, living in London, in the late 1990s, when she was well into her own 90s. She could look back on a wonderful career that saw her play piano or organ at many Southend venues, including the pier, and across Europe and South Africa. In her prime, so too was Southend in its prime as a resort and as a town in which permanently to reside. It had not yet been wearied by age and condemned by social rebellion.

When I was barely into my teens, I made up my mind to visit every one of the cinemas in and around Southend. I achieved target, always accompanied by one or another of my friends, always for afternoon shows on Saturdays or holiday times. We saved or earned the admission fee and walked to and from the theatres, except for those outside the borough boundary or the old Palace at Shoebury. The last-named, a camping showroom these past many years, had opened around the beginning of the Great War and thrived on the support of troops based at Shoebury Garrison and, then, the wives and families of the soldiers who settled locally and helped to build a largely-independent economy. The Palace finally closed in 1955, although the building of today is clearly recognisable as a former picture house.

I went there only once – and I ended the visit abruptly and in terror when with some shouted obscenity from a local youth seated immediately behind me, in reference to my being a stranger to the place, the lengthy blade of a sheath knife was thrust through the back of my seat, missing me by the narrowest of good fortune. I did not linger to see who had carried out this wicked deed, this rare act of chilling violence in an age when such incidents were relatively few. Shocked, horrified, scared as never before, I leapt to my feet, raced up the slightly-sloped aisle and burst through the doors and into the daylight and kept running, along Ness Road and to Shoebury Common, where buses from Southend turned for the return journey along the seafront.

I cannot remember now which of my pals was with me, but I know that when I shouted and dashed for safety, he ran like a hare, too. It seemed almost beyond belief, some made-up tale by two youngsters touched by the drama on the screen, so we kept the secret to ourselves, as though it was something shameful we had done. I remain most grateful that the impression it left on me was in the mind, not physical. I never did return to the Palace at Shoebury, though.

Thereafter, the nearest I went to it, to the flicks, in the east of the borough, was to the Plaza in Southchurch Road; and that was considerable distance from Shoebury, physically and in many ways. The Plaza is a community and religious centre at this time, after having been for some years an electrical warehouse. But for most of the first thirty years of its life after it opened in 1929, it was a cinema, with brief change to live repertory theatre. I recall that it had more than one-thousand seats and I also remember ordering a pot of tea and iced buns on arrival. This fare was delivered on a tray and thoroughly enjoyed at the interval.

In the year of the birth of the Plaza, 1929, the Rivoli in Alexandra Street, opposite the lovely old Victorian police station, with the courtrooms across the yard to the redbrick building's rear, introduced talking pictures to an incredulous public. This was somewhat before my time, and some years after the entertainment centre had opened in 1896 as the Empire, its name again in this new millennium when it stages live theatre. It was the Rivoli through my youth and we regularly queued through the alleyways on either side of the building, linking Alexandra Street and Clarence Street. By that ghastly decade of the sixties, it was rebuilt in the ugliness of that age and known as the ABC. Come the eighties it was twinned as the Cannon and eventually it closed and reverted to its present use for stage shows.

My own personal favourite of all the many cinemas was the Ritz, a wonderful and typical thirties building whose half-rounded front faced the Palace Hotel and dominated where, now, the multi-storey car park of this time and of the Royals mall, is a monument to change. I went for years to the Saturday morning club at the Ritz, with my pals. We walked through the byways and alleyways that led us from home to the narrow path that ends between St. John's church and the tiny yard behind the Palace Hotel. Roy Rogers on Trigger, Hopalong Cassidy and singing cowboy Gene Autry carried us with them on their trusty steeds into the Wild West – and Flash Gordon lifted us into the future in his rocketship. In the darkness, summer and winter, we were lost for three hours in and beyond a world of wonder and excitement.

And then, when we were so sophisticated and so grown up that we had our first long-trousered suits, we left the Saturday club to the kids and went to see the real, adult movies that sometimes showed men and women kissing each other and lighting cigarettes for each other and going hand-in-hand through a door while violin music soared to inspirational heights and old women around us, who were probably twenty-one or even more, sighed loudly.

The Ritz, with almost two-thousand seats, its own upstairs restaurant and ballroom, was born in 1935, a couple of years after me. Its death in the early 1970s was painful. It lingered through a time of bingo before its own number was called in controversial circumstances. Memory tells me that amid calls for its survival, professional wreckers turned up when no one else much was about: on a Sunday, I think. With modern equipment, the art deco haven of my formative years and many of my dreams was skittled like tenpins, with nothing much remaining for any to argue over by the time the papers got on to the story. This kind of thing has been an oft-repeated refrain in my lifetime in Southend.

The song ended for the mid-High Street Odeon in the 1990s, but the memories linger on. Is it any wonder, when this was the biggest and best of them all, the mother and father of all the cinemas of the 20th century? The year of 1935 was a very good year for Southend. Not only did the Civic, which became the Talza, which then became the New Vic, open at Victoria Circus, across from the Gaumont Palace; the Ritz opened above Pier Hill, or Royal Hill as it is actually named but hardly ever known, and the 3,000-seat Astoria with its Compton organ, its restaurant and its glittering entrance and stairways opened in high summer. It was to become the Odeon in 1944 and it was then to become the place where, on Sunday evenings especially, the youth of the town and around were to be seen and found.

The queues went in two directions from the High Street entrance and grand foyer, one tailing back towards Elmer Approach and to behind the theatre, the other stretching back beyond the High Street neighbours to where the road led to the Central station and then snaked back so that the tails of the two great lines met. Regulars knew at which point in any queue was the cut-off place for a guaranteed seat. Beyond this point, the patient patrons-in-waiting might get a standing-room only admission if they were lucky.

All the new, first-run films came to the Odeon. It was a considerable jewel in the Rank empire and every postwar summer for many years at carnival time, when Southend was packed and sizzling and wonderfully and peacefully alive and throbbing with excitement, some of the leading British film stars came to make personal appearances and to crown the new queen. It is not over-stating the story to report that these glittering occasions, when women wore posh frocks and men donned blacktie suits, were akin to

Hollywood first nights. Crowds pushed outside not only for seats, but for glimpses of the famous arriving. The glamour was such a thrilling contrast to the lingering austerity that stretched far into peacetime.

The Odeon had well-known, publicity-conscious managers of considerable personality over many years, all of whom I came to know through newspaper work: Teddy Pike, Alf Crisp, Arthur Levenson. Arthur's long reign in charge, when he won showmanship awards and applause galore, included a period through the 1960s when live stage shows were alternated with films and most of the star names of rock and pop music appeared here, including the Beatles in 1963. Back in the mid-forties, though, attendance records of tens of thousands were set when a film called The Best Years of Our Lives was the great and magnetic feature. I saw it more than once and I cried unashamedly each time. It starred Fredric March and Myrna Loy as a couple in smalltown America whose daughter waited and yearned to marry her childhood sweetheart when he came home from the Navy at war's end and he had lost both his hands, which were replaced with artifical limbs. It was tragic and it was beautiful and it was inspirational and it was moving in the extreme and it was in black and white and they don't make 'em like it any more, more's the pity.

But the stark and jolting reality of such fine films was soon to be overshadowed by the truelife drama of changing tastes and changing demands and changing options. Cinema as my generation knew and loved it, was oldtime for the new, television generation. And so, by 1970, long beyond my youth, the magnificent Odeon was briefly closed, divided into two much smaller theatres above a groundfloor supermarket. As such, as a shadow of its former self, the glamour given way to the functional, it lived on until the opening of the multi-screened Odeon of today. The film industry thrives on sentimentality and make-believe, but the entertainments business has little time for self-sentiment: it is ruled by financial figures more than by famous figures. And so, through my own years, Southend's cinemas were gradually felled without ceremony, cut down after their prime. I visited them all. I walked the London Road, from Vic Circus, to reach the Mascot, on the right a short distance beyond the Palace, a theatre which thankfully survives still after its own many ups and downs since its opening in 1912. The Mascot burned to the ground late one night in 1964 when a firework thrown by some hooligan during the evening performance, smouldered slowly and threateningly without being seen; and it started a small and unnoticed fire which became a raging inferno. They didn't bother to replace the cinema; a store eventually arose on the site.

Across the road, the town's most modern of cinemas, dating from 1939, the Metropole which became the Classic and, later, the Cannon, survived until the early 1990s and then was demolished for different redevelopment. In Leigh, the Corona had already been closed for some thirty years and the Coliseum for about twenty-five years.

Going West – as so many cinemas did, in time, so to speak – I first reached the Kingsway at Hadleigh, just beyond Southend's western boundary, around 1950. I was a local reporter and used sometimes to call-in at the independent theatre, which had opened in 1936 and whose architecture and interior design wonderfully represented that decade. It boasted a Compton organ and it had a manager named Gus Keeling. He looked like what he claimed to be, a veteran of Vaudeville. He was given to wearing loud check suits, suede leather shoes and a brown trilby worn at rakish angle. He often had a short fag-end in the corner of his mouth and he was just like many comics are said to be, away from an audience: he was gruff and short and miserable.

He once told me he had appeared at the turn of the century with a comic genius named Charlie Chaplin, but he never elaborated. When he retired the staff and a few locals gathered to say farewell. A uniformed commissionaire standing alongside me said in a stage whisper, words that have remained with me for some half a century, registered in my mind for their cruelty: "So that's it, then – the end of a long and useless career." The Kingsway ended its career a year or a few after Mr. Keeling. Well, it seemed as though it had done so, although it did eventually reopen and survived until around 1970, when its site became valuable and the final curtain on cinema fell ahead of the heavy ball at the end of the demolition experts' chain.

About that time, the Century facing the old London Road at Pitsea, just beyond the then famous open air market on the way to London, closed as a cinema and became a bingo emporium. It had become the Century in 1948, some eighteen years after it opened as the Broadway. Its earlier owners were the Howard's Dairies family, whose name and reputation were well-known across southeast Essex for decades. Also in the seventies, the Rio at Canvey dropped films and introduced bingo; while the Regal at Rayleigh was smashed down for new development to take its place.

I had sat at some earlier time in each and every one of them, conveyed magically and momentarily into different times, places, cultures and customs. Each, in its own way, had played a significant part in my childhood or my youth; each had provided adventure or romance, provoked laughter or tears. All were part of that wonderful world of make-believe into which we escaped in an age of simple pleasures and true gratitude.

A great, big, sophisticated, technically-advancing and shrinking world was waiting outside the cinema doors. The men in suits and office suites thought they were playing necessary roles in the New Order when they started to bring down the curtains, knock down the old picture palaces and make way for the great future. But what they did, was take away a whole way of life that would never again be the same. They replaced make-believe and myth with a material mass.

Those who arrived in the sixties and seventies will never know that they missed. It was wonderful.

13

OF course, what brought cinema to its knees, and left it there for many years, was television. And what, with extreme irony, helped to close so many picture houses in and around Southend was a Southend-based company, E. K. Cole Ltd., known worldwide as Ekco. It had started as a one-man band, grew into a mammoth employer locally and elsewhere, boomed through the golden years of radio and then, in the early 1950s, began to flood the market in meeting the fast-increasing demand for television sets.

My mother worked briefly on the Ekco production line at its main Southend factory in wartime, when women were encouraged to replace men who had gone off to serve in the Forces. My brother worked for many years in the drawing office. There were times, it seemed, when almost every family in the town had a member on the Ekco staff or knew someone who knew someone there.

By 1953, when the company had diversified into various areas and had contracts or contacts in many countries, its own publicity department published the numbers of employees at various locations as totalling 4,897. By far the most, of course, were at the main offices and factory in Priory Crescent, 3,213. Another 936 worked at Malmesbury, in Wiltshire, to where some production had been evacuated in wartime, and the remainder were shared between company premises on Canvey Island, in Hadleigh and in Southend. But as the introduction of Independent Television was still two years away, the real boom in TV viewing was yet to arrive.

As a boy I had been fascinated by the design of the Ekco wireless sets, which were our only real link to anywhere much beyond a few miles from home in Southend. The 1930s cabinets were moulded in a kind of advanced plastic, Bakelite, and turned out on huge presses in Germany. Similar machines were in time installed at the Southend main factory, producing the pleasing kinds of results that can be viewed to this day in a wonderful exhibition at the Priory Museum.

Also as a boy, cycling to and from a Southend High School separated from the Ekco main building only by the width of Priory Park plus a little, I was amazed by the numbers of workers who themselves went by bike. I had never, ever seen so many men and women pedalling in one place at one time, when they shared our roads with buses and a few cars; and I was not reminded of the bicycle spectacle until I went to Beijing in the 1980s and was astonished at the massed ranks of cyclists and the near-deafening chorus of ringing bells.

But I have moved too far ahead in this review of one of the most outstanding success stories of modern Southend, a story that interested me considerably for years and which took on even greater fascination after I exchanged letters with former headmaster Derek Cole, living in retirement in Sussex as this chapter was being written. For he is the son of Eric Kirkham Cole, the genius who gave his name and his brilliance to Ekco and saw it grow from back garden shed obscurity to international fame. Oh, yes – a remarkable story indeed.

Around 1920 Eric Cole, a physically small man, son of a milkman, was wiring houses in and around the Shaftesbury Avenue area of Southend, east of the gasworks and facing Southchurch Park, as electricity gradually took over from gas, and he often worked for a major developer named Henry James Manners, another of the many characters who helped to build Southend and the fascinating story of Southend. Manners, who was found dead in his bed at a luxury apartment at the Selsdon Country Club when I was a mere lad, had suffered a heart attack after an afternoon round of golf. His name lived on long after, in the partnership of Maxwell Manners Pring that had various interests in Southend, including ownership of the then

Boating Pool to the east of the pier, now part of the Miller family's Adventure Island complex. And the name survives to this time, in Manners Way, at Prittlewell, an extensive area of which Manners' company developed.

Eric Cole, in his spare time when not working for Manners or others, was intensely interested in the newfangled radio and, in a shed behind the family home in Beedell Avenue, Westcliff, he carried out various experiments. He had a great pal to help him with these and with electrical repairs that brought in some money, Stanley Clements. They also had among their customers a salesman named William Streatfield Verrells, or Billy Verrells as he was widely known; and when Verrells confirmed others' worries over the high cost of high-tension batteries then used in wireless sets, Cole invented a battery eliminator.

Much impressed, Verrells put a small financial stake into a partnership that became a limited company and began rapidly to grow towards public status, so that it moved to bigger and better premises including the old Gliderdrome amusements hall behind Eastern Esplanade at Thorpe Bay, mentioned earlier in this journal. Staff numbers also grew at a steady pace and with increasing sales and soaring profits, the Ekco's fine new offices and factory were built by 1930, with the firm of Henry James Manners contracted to carry out the work, on a twenty-acre open site at Priory Crescent, the factory floor area measuring 350,000 square feet.

Even a huge fire there within a year or so of its opening, proved only an interruption to the rise and rise of the Ekco fortunes. Derek Cole recalls, "My mother always said that my earliest participation in the Ekco business was when I was a few months old in 1931, the day the factory burnt down. The London newspapers persistently phoned her at our home in Thorpe Bay, waking me each time. As I was teething and howling endlessly, the hacks had some difficulty in hearing what she was saying."

Yet although Ekco had grown in a mere few years from a back garden enterprise to an organisation of immense fame and influence, often under the media spotlight, Eric Cole is remembered by his son as "a really most extraordinary man – very shy and diffident and reluctant to take responsibility, but at the same time he could not be pushed around." Derek Cole confirms that Eric tried for years to avoid running the company that bore his name and was not chairman until 1947. "He never owned the company, as the five founders split the shares almost equally in 1926 and for twenty years he thought of himself as the engineer, not the boss."

Derek explains that "although as a family we lived a comfortable enough life, he drew surprisingly little from the firm. His early partner, Billy Verrells, drew up contracts for them both in 1935 which entitled father to a car, chauffeur and good commission on profits. He had his Bentley and, indeed, employed a chauffeur, but as he always drove himself he paid the chauffeur out of his own pocket."

Ekco spread its considerable arms to embrace all kinds of developments and products as well as its famous wireless sets. It was heavily involved in war work, much of this concentrated in Wiltshire while Southend was seen as particularly vulnerable to enemy attack, and by now, with several factories in several parts of the country, the total workforce was around seven-thousand. As Eric Cole himself would say in the introduction to one of the company's glossy postwar brochures, "The Ekco story is of continuous growth and expansion, a story to which new chapters are being added every year." He listed its commitments to television, heating, electronics, nucleonics, radar, plastics, cinematography "on land, at sea, in the air, in this country and overseas."

By now, the commission on profits to which Cole was entitled had reached huge level – "He waived about £200,000, millions in today's money," recalls his son. "This caused consternation at the Inland Revenue, which tried to say he should pay tax on it as technically he had received it and handed it back! Such conduct by him was clearly outside the Revenue's experience and new Treasury forms had to be invented so that he could renounce the commission by deed." The company's silver jubilee was celebrated in 1951 and in grand fashion. A lavish banquet, followed by extensive entertainment, was held in the works dining room at Priory Crescent, another dinner was held at the Savoy Hotel in London, when the cabaret featured an up-and-coming newcomer named Tommy Cooper, and the whole staff, with partners, was invited to travel in specially-hired coaches to a specially-arranged performance of Rose Marie on Ice at the London Harringay Arena. On this occasion Eric Cole presented gold watches to four, including Stanley Clements, his old pal from the garden shed days, for their quarter of a century of service. Cole himself was presented with a portrait by Frank Salisbury "as a mark of employees' esteem and appreciation."

Although Eric remained a mostly shy and unassuming figure, he had considerable influence in Tory circles and personal connections at high level. Derek Cole, who was an active member of the old Southend West Liberal Party, certainly did not share his father's Conservative views. Derek is convinced that his father, with Sir Jules Thorn, of Ferguson, and C. O. Stanley, of Pye, were able to persuade the Conservative Government of the day to suddenly and surprisingly in the autumn of 1958 remove all restrictions on hire purchase and television rental. Ekco produced vast numbers of sets. And then the bubble well and truly burst. Stockpiles mounted in various factories and stores and warehouses in and around Southend.

Derek recalls that "the next budget saw further tax concessions and giveaways to win in 1959 an election which shortly before had seemed lost to the Conservatives. The consequences were disastrous for Ekco and the nation. After the election taxes went back up and and the Government imposed further restrictions on the television industry in April 1960 just as the recession in the industry began."

The great and heady years of the Ekco of Eric Cole were over. Derek Cole remembers that in that 1960 recession, when the company began to lay-off staff, his father stopped drawing his own salary. "Then," says Derek, "he resigned in disagreement with the policies of the newly-merged Pye-Ekco company. He had already let his contract expire so that the company owed him nothing. When the

Board offered him a golden handshake, he turned it down." More than thirty years on from the start of so remarkable a success story, Eric Cole left behind just about everything other than the name he had bequeathed, Ekco. He even lost his wife when she died in 1965. But little more than a year later, in November 1966, he was to rejoin her. He drowned while swimming in the West Indies on holiday. A permanent exhibition at Prittlewell of Ekco products, is scant recognition by the town of Southend of the life and times and contribution of Eric Kirkham Cole.

This writer has long wondered why no impressive memorial exists, naming and briefly detailing the life and times and contributions of those who have helped to shape Southend in that short timespan since the charter of borough status was granted in 1892. Eric's old friend from so long ago, Stanley Clements, stayed with the newly-married company until his own retirement, seven years after Eric's death. He was a widower, coming up ninety years old and living quietly in Hockley, when he too slipped away, a pioneer from an industry taken for granted in this technically-advanced age, but forged in the early twentieth century with considerable input, skill and entrepreneurial courage.

14

THE peak period for television production in Ekco's great years of the 1950s was from March to November. There were times when it seemed that as the fourteen-inch and fifteen-inch table or floor-standing models in the Ekcovision range came off the production line – 'Visual entertainment with a detailed clarity that cannot be surpassed' – there were lorries or customers waiting for them. But Stanley Clements, in his retirement, would recall that there would then be a rundown of staff until the next peak, the factory packed with workers on a Friday, almost empty on the Monday.

Even as a boy, even ahead of mass television ownership, I was aware of this kind of employment rollercoaster: the news of recruitment or layoff at the Ekco was for a long time a feature of local life. But its significance, its impact on the local economy and on individual homes, was far beyond the compass of childhood. In the wartime years, when we were all back from our safe havens in other parts of the country, and in the years into the fifties, there was much else to exercise young minds and bodies.

In the 21st century, when children spend so much time indoors, seated in front of computer screens and surfing websites, it will be almost impossible for anyone too young to remember the first half of the 20th century, to realise the extent of change. It will be inconceivable to many today, when children are taken by car to and from school and when parents fret and worry almost every time their offspring are out of sight, that the grandparents of now roamed free in their own innocent childhood: free from concerns over traffic, because it was sparse and slower, and free from fears of attack or abuse because crime and violence were minor compared to this age. The absence of personal transport lessened the possibility or risk of those of criminal intent travelling to unfamiliar surroundings; strangers in any localised community could be easily spotted and noted.

And so, after those early years of seldom moving outside our own tight community; of playing in the local park or on the local swings or swimming from the nearby beach, my friends and I began to stretch our longer legs as we aproached the start of the teen years. When I was about twelve years old, I formed a football team and called it Arnold Athletic. Its members went to Sunday School, often reluctantly so, it must be said, at the little outreach mission hut of St. Erkenwald's Church, at the corner of Arnold Avenue and Beresford Road, near where Southend United had its ground, at the edge of the Kursaal amusements park, until it moved to Grainger Road in the mid-1930s, and where the housing estate would rise in the 1970s after the Kursaal closed.

The Spanish-style, gigantic, thick-walled and entirely-brick St. Erkenwald's had risen in stages from the start of the 20th century, with a new parish created for it from 1910. There were rumours in the years I went there for special services, as a member of its Youth Club and briefly a Boy Scout, that it would become a cathedral when Southend became a city. It was an impressive landmark viewed from the Thames or from the pierhead, sharing the skyline with the Palace Hotel long before the town's designers and elected figures decided to try to turn Southend into some mini-Manhattan, with skyrise blocks to house council tenants and skyscraper offices to feed commercial appetite.

Alas for great ambitions, Southend did not attain city status and St. Erk's, as we knew it, did not survive as a church after 1977. Its congregations had dwindled and one of the later incumbents, the Reverend Joseph Lowe, whom many openly referred to as Holy Joe, had often upset the authorities by abandoning much tradition and holding community forums and chat sessions while also speaking out on issues that others might prefer to leave under the carpet or the altar cloth, such as the nuclear arms race and Third World poverty. Diocesan leaders eventually decreed that this particular church was redundant to needs and it was closed, its future uncertain for years until the inevitability of its 1990s demolition to make way for modern flats.

St. Erkenwald's had dominated at the corner of York Road and Southchurch Avenue through my young years. It must have been a part of Southend where regular worship was towards other than God, because it was not the only church to disappear. Facing it, at the other corner of the junction, had been the York Road Methodist Church, which succumbed to changes ahead of its neighbour and was knocked down some years earlier, to be replaced by flats. This had opened in 1898 and in the later stages of World War Two, when I went to evening meetings at St. Erk's, often the lights glowed in the semi-basement of the Methodist building and some of the thousands of troops who came and went in wartime Southend would be relaxing over tea, rock cakes and company in the canteen or playing such daring games as table tennis or billiards.

Nearby, a third church, Woodgrange Methodist, closed in 1952. This building, though, was not demolished. When the church congregation moved to new premises at Whittingham Avenue in Southchurch, the redundant building was sold to the Masonic movement and became a temple for that organisation, surviving still, its exterior largely unchanged since its first use in the 1920s, its interior familiar to those who practise the rites and rituals of freemasonry, but mostly a mystery to the rest of us.

But when these three churches in close proximity were still open and used by the faithful, so too was the little mission hut at the corner of the Kursaal grounds, south of the great Cyclone rail ride and at the eastern end of the extensive car park where charabancs were neatly lined-up in their hundreds in the seasonal boom times. Mr. Banks, who lived in one of the flats of the 1913-built Beresford Mansions at the extreme other end of this car park, a near-neighbour of the Bela Lugosi look-alike who haunts an earlier chapter of this log, was in charge of the Mission. He had piercing eyes behind bullseye glasses, neatly-clipped, iron-grey hair and a moustache whose ends were waxed and twisted into replicas of steel knitting needles. He also had much patience and understanding of children, though he and his wife had none of their own, as far as I know.

He encouraged our attendance on Sunday afternoons, by allowing us also to meet in the building on a midweek evening, when the chairs were pushed back to the walls, to enable us to play five-a-side football practice matches in the confined space. It was probably assumed by Mr. Banks that we would dress properly and behave properly and sing loudly and listen attentively on the Sabbath; and it was assumed by us boys that our ball skills on the highly-polished, linoleum floor of the hut would stand us in fine stead on the proper field of play. Our assumption was quite incorrect.

As the player-manager of Arnold Athletic, as well as the on-field captain, I led my twelve-year-old men into many a match or battle. Alas, I am haunted by the distant memory that we never won a single game. Nor did we manage to hold out for a draw. But, as my father had so often said, the world loved those who tried and trying and failing was better than not trying at all. Or something like that.

The game took us to new fields; not simply to fields, but to distant places where we had not previously ventured and possibly would not have ventured for decades, without the challenge of a football contest. Whenever I heard of a team that might be up for a challenge – or whenever a team heard of us and our penchant not only for defeat, but for absolute tousing – written contact was made, since there was no telephone in my home or in those of any of my teammates.

Our most distant away fixture was at South Benfleet. It was in prospect a thrilling, daring adventure. We had saved the necessary money for our return fares from Southend East to Benfleet and we had looked forward with increasing uncertainty and teeth-chattering anticipation to the Saturday afternoon meeting with a team reputedly regarded as a nursery for West Ham United. It began to rain heavily early in the week. It continued to rain on successive days and it was still raining when we climbed aboard the old steam train and it stuttered and clattered on what would be our fateful journey to a farflung destination, all the way through Southend, Westcliff, Chalkwell and Leigh to this little village where the creek snaked in on one side of Canvey Island and the hulks and bits of boats had long since laid down to die.

Instructions had been received by post on how to find the Recreation Ground on leaving the station, so we plodded through the heavy rain to where we could see the netless goalposts at each end of a sloping and partly waterlogged pitch, each of the two wooden frames leaning slightly towards us, having long since given up trying to stand tall against the prevailing southwest wind.

To our amazement, there was the utter luxury of a hut in which to change into our playing kit and to leave our clothes. It smelled of damp and was as cold as an audience unwilling to be entertained by a rookie comedian; but a man in a flat cap and aged raincoat to his ankles greeted us warmly. As the father of one of the boys in our host team and the manager, he was amazed to meet the player-manager-skipper of the day's opponents – me. He was possibly even more surprised when we trotted out, hunched against the wind and rain, for we wore an assortment of shorts, socks, shirts and boots: owning a club strip was something we had not even dreamed of.

Of course, when the home side appeared they were in immaculate, matching kit. It was quickly apparent that they were as smart at the game as in their appearance. We rarely broke out of our own half of the field, not even after we changed ends and the wind was behind us. It wasn't simply that we were bogged down in ankle-deep mud; no, the boys of Benfleet who saw themselves as future West Ham stars were fitter, faster, stronger and far better organised than us. Well, we weren't organised at all, tell the truth. So we lost. Actually, we were thrashed. I cannot recall that we had one single shot at their goal. They had far too many at ours for anyone to count. Of these, nineteen went between our posts.

When it was over, when the man in the raincoat and flat cap had blown the final whistle, for he acted as the referee, too, the two teams shook hands and we trudged wearily back to the hut, to don our going-home clothes over our mud-caked football togs. Our hosts had given us three cheers, as was the custom at the end of most amateur matches then, and Mr. Flat Cap had come into our changing area to thank us and to wish us well. He must have been a wonderful father and a man with a golden heart, because he said we had played well in very difficult circumstances and even though we had lost, our team had provided the Man of the Match, in his opinion. He said it was me and he shook my hand and I headed for the train tired, soaked, body wracked by aches, smothered in mud, yet glowing with pride because I could not for a moment imagine that this man had meant anything other than what he said.

We never again suffered so heavy a defeat. I am not even sure, now, that any other team managed to beat us by double-figures, though it is distinctly possible. We played our home matches at Southchurch Park, when the proper, grown-up teams were not booked for the one pitch there, alongside Kensington Road, and when we had between us saved enough in the kitty to pay for the hire. The council's Parks Department was based, then, in Burdett Road, just off the seafront, close to my home, and I would visit the front office to find a vacant date, hand over the cash and obtain a receipt for day and time. Memories are of a ground that seemed always rock hard, so that the ball bounced like a delinquent beyond control and playing in goal, as I often did, meant diving around on a surface akin to concrete. This, and our lack of funds, ensured that most of our matches were away from home territory.

We walked one Saturday from the Kursaal to the great bus park area alongside Victoria Station, already dressed in our ragbag of outfits beneath topcoats, but carrying our boots, and caught a bus to another distant and strange place called Ashingdon. On this occasion, as in the bog of Benfleet, I appeared at left-half, having been inspired by the performances from this position of the Tottenham and Wales captain, Ronnie Burgess, of whom I read as much as possible in as many newspapers as I could come across. I hoped I might captain and lead my men to some gloriously memorable achievement. In the event, all I can remember is leaving our coats and shoes under a hedge in time for the kick-off and retrieving them before returning home after the village boys had given the townies yet another lesson. Likewise, we returned home humbled from a fixture at Shoebury Park, which appeared at that time to be in some wild and largely uninhabited, remote part of the British Isles.

We cycled to this match, about three miles from the Mission Hut where we had gathered, along the seafront to Shoebury Common, round into Ness Road and then to Elm Road, a country lane with the occasional detached bungalow along its edges, and over the railway bridge. The waiting natives did not seem at all friendly. There were no changing facilities and not even goal posts.

Sticks had been hammered into the ground at the nominal four corners of the pitch and to identify each end of each goal. I had returned to my goalkeeping position, since England's Frank Swift was my role model hero of that week, and I wore the secondhand green, rollnecked woollen jersey I had obtained from a boy named McLeod, whose father ran a private school in Southchurch Road, in exchange for a penknife or something equally valuable and cherished. The jersey had several holes other than those at the neck and wrists and might well have been a horse blanket in a previous life because I had to roll back the sleeves so many times, they were like car tyres at my elbows and the hem reached to my knees.

Unfortunately, I was not of the size or talent of Mr. Swift, so the ball was kicked past me or over me numerous times in the siege of Shoeburyness and, as there were no goal posts and therefore no nets, I spent much of the afternoon retrieving the leather sphere from distant parts of the arena. I became thoroughly exhausted; and so, with no referee, no whistle and no watch between the twenty-two of us from the two teams, I decided this was more cricket match than football match when the score had mounted, and I declared. I declared that enough was enough and the game was over.

We hobbled slowly to pick up our bikes from where they lay on the ground and, to a chorus of laughs and jeers from our hosts, we rode in the direction of civilisation. Arnold Athletic sort of went west around that time, too; more disbanded than demoralised, one likes to think.

15

THERE were lots of things for adventurous boys to do, and never mind the football playing, in the post-evacuation war years and after we had celebrated the end of hostilities with our street parties. There were the cliffs gardens to explore, to use for games of hide and seek that went on until boredom or frustration at failure to locate quarry in the thick undergrowth, prompted unanimous agreement to do something else. Oh, yes – we sometimes also learned a little about the kind of games played by grown-ups in the long grass or beneath some particularly bushy spot away from the pathways.

There were many soldiers, sailors and airmen in Southend then; and plenty of American sailors and troops. There were lots of teenage girls, too, and young women whose menfolk were away, long gone oversees, the present as uncertain as the future. So, in the cliffs gardens, in our innocent games of tracking or playing detectives, there were times when we saw and heard couples who were locked intensely in their own shared moments, oblivious to passersby or to inquisitive little boys. We could not know, not back then, that maybe some of those who were living for the moment, might well have been someone else's wife or someone else's husband and that at such a desperate and terrible time, they shared illicit meetings because they needed to be needed and they could not predict when, or even if ever, such moments would arise again.

We saw and we heard things that were not considered the province of youngsters in an age when we knew very little; and when we went about our own make-believe and far more important business of staging our own adventures. We shaped broken twigs as arrowheads and left them in the centres of paths to point those who came to seek us, after an agreed time delay, in the direction we had taken. We might snag a piece of paper on a low branch or chalk a mark somewhere. Sometimes, the pursued would hide, silent and almost as frightened of discovery as men tracked by enemy, until the pursuers had passed. Then the hunted became the hunters. The games would continue for half a day, maybe even a whole day if we had taken with us some sandwiches and bottled drink, packed into the rucksacks of the few from the many who had such equipment.

There were times, when the seafront finally was opened up in peacetime after the years of barbed wire and barricades and barred access, we would trek and track in those wonderful public gardens from the old Calcutts pub, next to the Cliffs Lift, all the way to the fenced-off Shorefields area. Here, through the cracks or gaps in the fencing, we could see where, before the war, work had been started on what was known as the Shorefields Pavilion and would, when resumed and finally opened in the second half of the century, be named the Cliffs Pavilion. Towering concrete posts stood to attention in the footings, the reinforcing rods as twisted as the weeds that entangled the abandoned workings.

There were hot and sunny days when we queued to get into the Westcliff Swimming Bath, now the site of the seafront casino and restaurant, then a fabulous attraction whose charms and customers faded into history by the late sixties. The great, heated pool, its tiled bottom and sides seen from the prom above or from seats in viewing areas at road level through clear and shimmering water, boasted considerable measurements of some 300 feet in length and 70 feet across, from shallow to very deep at the end where waterchutes, springboards and tiered diving boards waited for the daring or the showoffs to flex muscles and demonstrate their range of diving, leaping or twisting, turning, somesaulting and plunging skills

Open-railed iron gates fronted the concrete steps that led from the Esplanade to the below-the-road turnstiles and admission to this watery and wonderful world. The pool was ringed by perhaps two-hundred little cubicles in which to change into swimwear and to leave one's clothes. They stank unpleasantly and the wooden-slated duckboards on the concrete floor were slippery and slimy. We changed as speedily and carefully as possible, leaving clothes on a shelf or wall pegs and stepping out hurriedly into the warmer and much fresher air. We wore woollen trunks, as boys: none of your fancy and colourful shorts and cutaways of another age. The girls were in dull, long, one-piece costumes that left nothing to admire but covered curves.

Numbered tags, to be tied to wrists or to waistbands, were issued on arrival. When the pool became particularly packed and the queue for new admissions was long, attendants shouted numbers through loud hailers. If your number was up, your time was up. Amazingly, now, one recalls that those summoned to leave the pool, change and vacate the sentry box-like cubicles, did as they were told. There were no untoward or unpleasant incidents in my recollections of countless visits to this grand, open-air pool that had been popular since soon after the First War and, now, beyond the Second.

It was only pure wicked and unfounded rumour when, often, boys leaving the pool would sidle up to those waiting to go in, to whisper a warning, "Don't try the waterchutes. Someone has lined their edges with razor blades. You'll be cut to pieces." The dire news would spread like butter under a blowlamp. Only when one entered through the turnstiles and saw others plunging happily and without injury down the water-flushed slides and into the deep end, would the rumour be seen as just that.

There were often rumours, too, of the spreading of some horribly contagious, ghastly and truly terrifying infections as a result of stepping barefoot into one of the cubicles or sharing the pool with unclean individuals among the hundreds swimming and diving and splashing and frolicking in the water, but I never experienced any kind of illness or problem and never knew of anyone else who suffered in any way. But in wartime, when so many terrible things happened or so many dreadful threats and possibilities often seemed imminent, rumours tended to spread like the plague. As we approached our teens, word went round that boys who had anything to do with certain kinds of girls would end up with the most horrifying of diseases so that bits and pieces would fall off the body. Just occasionally, when we were out and about in numbers, we would keep eyes open for any of these certain kinds of girls, but we never saw any we recognised as being in any way different or dangerous. All this was ahead of mass innoculation, of course, so that the likes of diphtheria, whooping cough and polio were still virulent diseases with the threat and dreadful potential of an unseen enemy.

One of the few diseases that had not taken hold in any widely recognisable way was vandalism. This would reach epidemic proportion much later, with no apparent remedy or cure. But back in wartime and just after, we climbed tall trees for the sheer fun and challenge and for the view, but we did not break branches. We shinned other trees to scrump the occasional apple. We hid in bushes and gardens and undergrowth, but we did not maim or destroy.

And as we grew older and bolder, so we went on truly challenging expeditions. We cycled to Hockley Woods, behind the centuries-old Bull Inn, and made our way deep in the dense growth, silent and alert, Errol Flynn and his men tracking down the unseen, wicked enemy depicted for us on the cinema screen and in the newsreels. On other forays we sneaked through the thickets below the Hadleigh Downs, having marched from Leigh Station, then spread out, to creep and crawl, duck and run from various directions towards Hadleigh Castle. Up there, we knew for sure in our minds, there were lookouts trying desperately to ensure that the towers and the keep and those therein could not be attacked, unawares. Those of the 13th and 14th centuries who had kept watch here, commanding a view of the entire Thames Estuary, ever prepared for landings by those dastardly French, had it easy compared with the lot of any 20th century successors who might try to detect us boys from Southend.

We were patient and painstaking in our approach up those steep slopes, snaking through the long grass, stopping regularly to look and to listen. When we did see strangers, they were more in our minds than anywhere else. When we made it to the base of the biggest of the great, surviving towers, any quarry had long since fled. The place was ours, to explore and to climb, to rest and to refresh ourselves with sandwiches and lemonade before the long trek back to the railway station or to meet yet another challenge such as a hike round the seawall, way out beyond the flat marshlands, to Benfleet.

This was a favourite. For still, as the war moved to its wonderful end and the second half of the 1940s began, there were occupied houseboats moored along Benfleet Creek: a fascinating hamlet of old boats and barges amateurishly or professionally extended and converted into a mass and a mess of hovels and handsome homesteads reached from the shore by dinghy or linked to the shore by rows of rickety wooden jetties. Some of these weird craft still floated on the tide when it flooded into the creeks and covered the saltings. Others had long since given up any pretence of seaworthiness and had settled into the mud and settled into a new and most unusual way of life.

If speculation or innuendo was to be believed, they were peopled by cranks or queer folk, because anyone different from the so-called normal has always been demented or dangerous or to be avoided or suspected. The reality, as we would learn when we grew up, was that homeless folk in the wake of World War One had squatted in old and abandoned craft or brought their own little vessels from the creeks and cuts off the lower Thames and elsewhere and, gradually, a little village had developed so that, by the early 1930s, the houseboat colonies had grown like the air of magic and mystery that surrounded them as surely as cold fog in deep winter.

Many were turned more into bungalows than boats, with rooms built below decks and added above decks. They were lit by oil lamps and meals were cooked on oil stoves. Those residents who bathed, did so in the tidal waters – though one hesitates to linger over any consideration of the emptying of human and other waste into the outgoing tide. The colonies became so established, down the years, that tradesmen called with groceries and milk and bread. In time, even the postman arrived on his rounds. Fresh water was sold from homes nearby and poured into containers on the houseboat homes.

The charm and magnetism of so unusual a community naturally attracted those with nose for news. The old Sunday Dispatch, which would go the way of many newspapers in the late 1950s, into oblivion, sent a man down the Thames in the winter of 1934 to look into the story, prompted by the knowledge that sanitary inspectors were unhappy over hygiene fears, local councils were unhappy about not getting any rates or rents and the Port of London Authority, which claimed authority over the Thames and almost everything to do with it, was unhappy that it had no hold over the mysterious and independent boat-dwellers of Leigh and Benfleet.

Amid such widespread unhappiness, the intrepid reporter communicated with head office from the 'water-villas in the Streets of Lost Ships.' Washing fluttered in the breeze from lines that stretched from boat to shore, he wrote, and practically every vessel boasted a wireless mast. He interviewed a Mr. Stace, a player of French horn and cello, who had gone up the creek with his wife and children following a slump in the music business and who reported, 'It's healthy here and it is cheap.' The scribe also spoke to various other dwellers whose names he withheld from publication: a young salesman recovering from a nervous breakdown, two artists, a retired sailor and some City office workers who each morning walked the dyke to Benfleet station and their commuter train, returning in the evening to their own piece of Paradise.

The man from the Dispatch popped-in on the Palmers' floating confectioner's shop at Leigh, was deterred by an Alsation dog guarding the Taj Mahal houseboat of a retired Indian civil servant, where Indian brassware could be seen behind the windows, and even discovered one moored mansion of a place with leadlight windows, mahogany doors and a drawbridge.

Most of these had gone, their residents finally forced out or moved elsewhere by Authority, by the time of our ventures to these parts that few youngsters then reached. But there were at Leigh some houseboats still to see, abandoned and rotting, victims of time and tide, and there were many skeletons of vessels lying in the mud, their frames reaching up like giants' ribs, the flesh long since picked from the bones. Further west, beyond the Southend boundary and in a spot more remote from any neighbours or officials, many houseboats were still occupied and would be, until into the 1950s. Some were proud, some pathetic; some miserable, some majestic.

Occasionally, as we headed along the embankment, inquisitive and tiring little lads making for Benfleet station and a train back to Southend East, a million miles away, someone would nod or wave to us from deck or window. Sometimes, when it seemed there might be no one else but us anywhere near, smoke from a stack on a boat would indicate human life aboard. We would pass dozens of these isolated homes that nestled together in an assortment as rich and varied as a box of Bassett's finest.

Between the wars, along the riverfront at Leigh and Benfleet, there had been some two-hundred houseboats. After the Second War they had dwindled into double figures, most at Benfleet. And then, as with so much of our boyhood and youth, they had disappeared because they did not fit into planners' blueprints and busybodies' acceptance; they did not conform and they had to go. The houseboats of Leigh and Benfleet sailed into history or were sunk without trace.

16

DEAR old, lovely old, wonderful old Southend pier would also come close to disappearing without trace, long after my first childhood and as I approached my second, because where there are countries and cultures that respect and protect the elderly, in our own land there is a tradition of ignoring the aged, presumably in hope or belief that they will simply fade away or go away.

The pier was of quite splendid seniority, well beyond its centenary, when those responsible for its welfare and its wellbeing became guilty of dereliction of duty. They more or less gave up on the poor old soul, assuming her deepening illness to be terminal; and in any case, with the arrival of the 1960s and the mass exodus of holidaymakers to more distant places than Britain's own seaside resorts, the reign of Alec White, whom we met earlier in this journal, was approaching its finale. His time as the town's entertainments mastermind and his service as chairman of the Pier and Foreshore Committee, spanning from a couple of years ahead of the war until decades after it, was ending. There was no strong and commanding and believing figure to champion an attraction that no longer attracted paying customers in even a fraction of the numbers of yore.

But long ahead of this cavalier and callous disregard of an asset that played so prominent a role in bringing the town its first fame and fortune, the pier was in blooming fine health when war was over and it had returned to peacetime duties and I was just into my teens and in love with the old lady. Well, you couldn't help adoring the pier, if you were born near it and lived through its great years and its war service and when it was even more popular than any overnight sensation or instant wonder might become for future generations.

I think I made my debut as a pier supporter when I was about four years old. The older of my two brothers, some nine years my senior, was an avid fisherman by then. He spent hours and days at the pierhead, with his sandwich lunch in brown paper bag, catching the occasional dab or flounder to take home to mother, and probably dreaming that one day he would sail away on the kind of liners that used then to come downriver from the London docks and from Tilbury, beginning the great voyages that ended in faraway lands. An early memory is of journeying with my mother to the end of the pier in one of the open-sided trains, the toastracks as they were called, that had arrived with the opening of the new iron structure in 1889 and would not be replaced until the advanced, enclosed, London Underground-style cream and green models of 1949.

But it was after the war, when the pier had reopened following distinguished military service, in that great revival period of our nation's resorts, that I really fell for the old girl who had survived so many indignities. To walk the pier was to escape from the confines of my own small neighbourhood and from Southend itself, because leaving the shore to cross mudflats or the tide, was to distance oneself from land, as though on a cruise. The air was certainly different out there, a quarter of a mile, half a mile and, then, a mile and more into the estuary; and the atmosphere was intoxicating for a youngster amid the seething masses of people, coming or going, all released briefly from their own insular backgrounds, surroundings and inhibitions and exposed not only to the sea breezes and fresh air and heady mixtures of passengers on some expensive cruise, but to a rare freedom from the everyday world.

People sang and danced and laughed as might those released from longterm sentence; for, in a sense, that is exactly what they were. The long and trying and debilitating and sapping war was finally over, even if rationing and restrictions and reservation remained. We had survived it. And, here and now, there was brief escape from bombed and bedraggled London and from overcrowding and workaday routine.

In the second half of the 1940s, the end of Southend Pier was as close as its millions of visitors would get to the invigorating, daring, exotic and adventurous. It was hypnotic and it was heavenly. And if the mood and the magnetism could capture and hold so many grown-ups, local as well as those come by charabanc, train, paddle steamer or even on bicycles, it was utterly captivating to this Southend native, naive as any young teen of the pre-television age. Sometimes alone, occasionally with parents, mostly with pals – and, yes, to confess it this lifetime later, sometimes for free via a devious method of entry – I spent more time on the pier than I could ever recall.

Sometimes we tried to keep up for as long as possible with a toastrack train, running alongside it until exhausted or winded. Sometimes we asked the time as we left the shore and part-ran, part-walked in imitation of that distinctive and exaggerated gait of the professional walker, to the far-end station. Then we would again inquire of the time, to check whether we had failed to match, or hopefully bettered, a previous performance. Sometimes we walked backwards for many yards, eyes to the shore, hoping to avoid bumping into anyone making the return walk from the pierhead. Sometimes, on the most violently windy days, we would try physically to lean as ridiculously far forward and into the gale as possible, holding the most exaggerated of gravity-defying positions before falling to the decking.

Such little things did indeed please little minds, while keeping us happy, healthy, occupied, out of mischief and out at sea. And on summer days and in holidays and on weekend days, we would stand for ages, out near where the rail tracks ended, leaning on the railings and gazing down on the works of sand artist Bill Robinson, whose broad canvas was a great stretch of sandbank which was exposed at an early moment of the tide's departure and still uncovered until a late stage of its return. With combs, sharpened sticks, pieces of wood from which the sharpened ends of nails protruded, Bill drew the most wonderful of images that drew the applause and the tossed coins of appreciative viewers.

In his blue crew-necked jersey, his blue serge trousers rolled to the knees, feet bare and head covered by a peaked cap, the boatman and fisherman, part-time artist, literally scratched a living in the tourist season. Maritime scenes were his speciality. Great sailing ships, full-rigged, spinnakers billowing like huge pot bellies, running before a following strong breeze, raced through choppy seas, beneath clouded skies.

As he bent to his work, the scenes took shape to applause and cheers: lines, then details, then shading. He usually included in his considerable display, a detailed sketch of Westminster Abbey, too.

Bill was from down our way, from Arnold Avenue, beneath the shadow of the gasholders. He was of one of the many branches of Robinson in Southend, many associated with the sea. I never saw him without his cap or in anything other than fisherman's jersey and, often, in great thigh boots folded down to knee height. He had a son, Bill Junior, who was a heavyweight handy with his fists and rumoured in the late 1940s to have been spotted as a potential boxing pro; but he became a foreshore inspector instead and did duty for years along the seafront where his father and kinfolk of the Robinson clan made their living. Bill Junior made a premature departure to the Other Side, suddenly gone from our view as the wonderful drawings of his late father when the incoming tide wiped out a day's work on the sandbank.

Another branch of the Robinsons, Albert and his wife, son Eric and daughter Marjorie, lived a few doors from Bill and family in Arnold Avenue. Unusually and most surprisingly, for the folk from our community in those years from the mid-forties into the next decade, Albert had another home, too – at the end of the pier. He was berthing master when the pier was run like some great, ocean-going liner, with a master, assistants, engineers and staff. Because Albert had to be on duty or on standby at all hours, to ensure the safe and smooth docking or departure of the many ships that came and went in those times, he was given by the council a three-bedroomed house where, now, there is the pierhead pub just beyond and to the right of the rail station.

Majorie Robinson was a young woman when the family lived a mile from the shore. She used to travel on the pier train, then climb Pier hill and walk through the High Street to a secretarial job. One Saturday evening, when she went to the Ritz cinema at the top of the hill, overlooking the pier, she was approached by a polite young man who introduced himself as Len Fuller. He would become one of the best-known of amateur footballers, referees and officials and would also become her husband until he died suddenly, long beyond their ruby anniversary. Len thought Marj was joking when she agreed that he could walk her home, then said she lived on the pier. He quickly discovered the truth.

They strolled from the front doors of the Ritz, crossed the road and passed the main entrance of the then majestic Palace Hotel, went down a flight of stone steps, then over the roadway to the pier's entrance. The man on duty greeted Marj, then let her through. In future, Len was going to have to take the new light of his life back from their dates to catch the last pier train by eight on winter evenings or ten in summer. Unless they walked, of course. Which they did, often. But any lingering in shelters for a quick kiss or cuddle along the way was brief, because the shore-end duty officer would also buzz Albert Robinson at the pierhead house to let him know his daughter was safe and sound and on the way home.

Albert escorted his daughter on a specially-polished and gleaming pier train, fitted with mayoral cushions for the occasion, when Marj set off to marry Len Fuller in 1951 at the church of St. John the Baptist, behind the Palace Hotel. Pier staff, resplendent in dark uniforms with their double rows of brightly-polished buttons, cap covers of brilliant white, formed a guard of honour. It was another memorable day to add to the countless wonderful recollections of the pier.

Yet the world-renowned landmark, survivor of storms, fires, wayward vessels and much else, had come close to being substantially erased only a year or two before the Robinsons took up their unusual residence. The war in Europe was only seven months from its end. At around ten minutes before seven on the morning of October 11 in 1944, a great and thunderous and terrifying sound echoed around the shore end of the pier, its shuddering waves reaching out over a wide area to shake houses and buildings. I was awakened as the very bed in the downstairs room where I slept, in the road just behind the seafront, shook violently. Then there was silence; eerie, unbroken silence and, as an eleven-year-old, the incident faded quickly from my mind. If the grown-ups talked about it, I did not hear or comprehend.

Later, very much later, I was to learn that one of those new and most unbelievable of weapons, the V2 rocket, had plunged to earth a few yards west of the pier, above the hollow that housed the Peter Pan's Playground since the 1920s. This unmanned and indiscriminate, monstrous missile, whose existence was denied by the Government in a bid to maintain public morale and to try to mislead the Germans who launched them from the Continent, was among the first of many of these insidious weapons to land on southern England that autumn. We would also know, in time, that several others ended up in various parts of southeast Essex.

If that rocket, one of several recorded on October 11 alone, had fallen perhaps fifty or so yards short, it would have demolished the pier pavilion (which, as it turned out, would survive another fifteen years until a peacetime arsonist burned down the Victorian building). As it was, the pavilion was damaged and the shock waves from the great blast ripped out windows and removed roof tiles considerable distances away, while bits of the white-hot metal from the rocket's supersonic orbit, spattered over a wide area.

But the dear old pier had survived, as it had withstood aerial attack early in the war and as it had lived through the threat of planned, self-destruction from the hidden explosives in its structure, laid and primed ready for detonating if the strategic and important landmark fell into enemy hands. It reopened in mid-May 1945 and, as Alderman Henry Bride, much later to become the town's mayor, said in a little booklet published at the end of that decade by the

Corporation of Southend-on-Sea, "Never before had it been so popular; during 1949 more than three-million paid for admission, while the pier railway carried more than four-million passengers."

It was, for sure, popular with me and with several of my pals. We strolled among the hundreds who sat in rows in their deckchairs, grilling themselves as they slumbered in the sunshine; we wandered the arcades, watching people play the pintable machines; made faces at ourselves in the Hall of Mirrors; viewed the masses arriving or leaving on the various passenger vessels that linked Southend with London, Gravesend, the Medway, Herne Bay, Margate and, in time, Calais and Boulogne.

In those years when the war and its impact began slowly to distance itself from immediate thought, like bubbles fading in the wake of a steadily-moving ship, the pier helped also to broaden the view of life of a boy approaching young manhood. I had gone with my mother and aunts and my older brother, Peter, to celebrate his twenty-first birthday at a matinee performance of Ivor Novello's Dancing Years at a theatre in the Strand. Weaned and raised on wireless entertainment, on talks and quizzes and comedy shows and music, I suddenly tasted live theatre and loved it, as I thrilled also to after-show tea at the Lyon's Corner House. Ah, such sophistication, such lavish experience.

So, back in Southend, there was live entertainment at the pierhead, whose chronology now escapes me, but whose impression was lasting. At different times, in those heady years, one could listen to the splendid Ben Oakley Orchestra, hear the delightful piano playing in the tea rooms of Nancy Mount, whose sister Peggy went from Westcliff's Palace Theatre to considerable fame in films and on the London stage, or sit through grand summer shows such as Bubbles, Out of the Blue, Zip-A-Hoy. They may have been corny, by today's demands, but I don't think so. They were colourful and clean and cosy and reassuring because, now in peactime, they re-established what many thought had gone forever, back in 1939.

The pier's centenary had been celebrated in July 1935, when I was a two-year-old. Its dramatic role from 1939 was told by historian A. P. Herbert in a sellout book The War Story of Southend Pier. Later, one of the old lady's other famous admirers, Sir John Betjeman, would be quoted time and again for his view that "The pier is Southend, Southend is the pier." I had felt this from my earliest years of understanding, long before Sir John echoed so wide a belief, and as I grew up in Southend it never occurred to me that the pier would go into the kind of decline that arrives with old age.

17

WHENEVER I returned to shore from a day on the pier, or when I strolled the seafront, I lingered at the foot of Pier Hill to study one of the most amazing of sights – the sizzling sausages, bubbling baked beans and mountains of mashed potatoes in the window of Manning's eatery. Across many summer seasons, even though I never stepped through the door and never actually fancied the food that fed the milling and willing masses, to see it behind the shop window from the footpath was truly fascinating.

White-aproned men with hairy arms and great serving spoons scooped large dollops of white and fluffy potatoes, beans, and fat and greasy bangers from the immediately-behind-the-windows bain-marie on to thick, white plates to meet the seemingly insatiable demand of customers seated at marble-topped tables. From early morning until late into the evening, the great metal containers were replenished.

The potatoes, heaped in small mountains, gave off steam like miniature volcanoes threatening to erupt. The beans heaved and spluttered in the way of hot springs. The sausages slowly browned and crispened, as bodies under artificial tanning lights. I often tried to imagine, as I stood as though mesmerised, face close to the pane, how many tons of spuds were peeled and boiled and mashed with milk and butter in a season; how many cans of beans were heated; and how many of the thousands of sausages cooked here over the years might be needed in one great string to reach from the shore to the pierhead. I also admit, looking back such a long, long time, that I often wondered how many, if any, of the flies that sometimes flitted up and down the inside of the window might end up in those pans. Not too many people appeared to worry too much about such things, back then, when much else of far greater threat had been survived.

Manning's was a must for generations of visitors. It had begun life as Zanchi's sausage and mash parlour early in the 20th century. The name was advertised boldly high above the shop, on the flank wall of the nextdoor building, the end of that wonderful row of Regency houses whose upper floors, thankfully still with us when so much has been wilfully removed, identify their history even if the groundfloor fronts are of coarse character as befits the Golden Mile. But the Zanchi of old photographs had given way to Manning in my early years of wandering this area and Manning would be there for years until, at some time I no longer recall, it had gone, the last of such mammoth, mouthwatering and magnetic meals cooked and served, their like suddenly subservient to Big Mac and similar newcomers from other lands.

So what did we eat, before the Takeaway Age arrived, before Southend had any Indian or Chinese restaurants and collect-your-own meals of foreign origin? What were our meals in the 1930s, when so many people struggled to make ends meet, and in wartime, when most restaurants closed and when food was so strictly and severely rationed? How ever did we survive without burgers and barbies, pizzas and pasta, kebabs and curry, ribs and rice? Well, we did all right, thank you. What we ate might have been repetitive and boring, had we known anything different and by comparison with today's international cuisine and food fads that change more frequently than a politician's stance or the British weather, but we are here still to tell the tale, right?

We had faggots, didn't we? And rissoles. Well, I didn't. The very names did not appeal to my Dad, so such concoctions of minced meat and herbs were not part of the menu in my boyhood home, even if they were cheap and popular elsewhere. Down our way, when the boats came in or old Tommy Nash passed by with his barrow, we had lots of fish. When this was less easily available we had plenty of inexpensive, filling meals that would not at all appeal to fashion models shaped like broom handles – suet puddings laced with chopped onions and sprinkled with bits of bacon; roly-poly, jam-filled steam puds; mammoth stews of mostly vegetables, a few pieces of meat and dumplings the size of cricket balls; toad-in-the-hole, the occasional lonely sausage baked in a great sea of Yorkshire pudding mix.

In wartime, when rationing decreed we may have about one pound of meat for each person each week and a mere four ounces of bacon, the Americans did not only send us their soldiers and sailors with their gum and their nylons and their roving eyes and hands. Nor would these wealthy, easygoing, smartly-uniformed, film star-like guys be remembered by the girls merely as wonderful jitterbuggers and known by envious young Englishmen as minus the jitter. No, the Yanks also brought us – or, rather, shipped to us – dried, powdered egg when we hardly ever saw one of the real, freshly-laid or even dated, shelled variety.

I have no record or recollection of what may have been any consensus view of dried egg, but I loved it. Mixed with milk or water, poured into a pan of shallow fat and fried, then flipped over pancake-fashion, it made a wonderful substitute for a fried egg, a kind of flapjack omlet delicious as sandwich filling.

And then, from across the Atlantic, came the Spam. Supply Pressed American Meat. Now, maybe it would lead to that classic Monty Python sketch of the late sixties, but back then it helped to fill our plates. The solid chunk of pink pork luncheon meat in a tin, or a can as the Americans have it, was a succulent saviour. We ate it in cold slices, with mashed spuds and pickles or cabbage or anything our mothers could manage to grow, borrow, barter for or buy. We ate it hot, after it had been shallow-fried in dripping or just about any kind of fat that might be available. Then there was the great speciality, the Spam fritter. Slices of the meat were dipped in thick, glutinous flour-mix then dropped into deep and boiling oil or fat and cooked until golden brown.

Delia, Pru, Anton, Gary boy, the Roux brothers or even young Jamie might not approve, in the age of food fads and millionaire chefs and more cookery programmes and books than hot dinners, but us survivors of rationed food and rationed finances knew a thing or two about a good nosh of Spam or boiled beef, carrots and pease pudding or baked rabbit or rabbit pie or shepherd's pie that had caught only a glimpse of the shepherd, if at all. We knew enough and scraped together enough to be able to reject the whale meat steaks that a deluded, if well-intentioned, government tried to encourage the population at large to accept.

For seconds, dessert, sweet or afters – after the filling main meal of the day, that is – we consumed great (and this refers to quantity before quality) dishes of tapioca, a frogs'-spawn-like mess; baked rice puddings under thick and brown top skin, well laced with jam of any variety when it was available; semolina, the hard and long-boiled grains of flour; Manchester tart, a thick pastry base spread with watered-down jam and topped with custard; Spotted Dick steamed puds; fruit- or jam-filled suet puddings that were steamed for hours. The range of choices, the ingenuity in straitened times and often in hard-up homes of that period, was quite astonishing.

Today's gourmets and instant experts, the everyday sophisticates who have travelled the world and taste-tested international cuisine or stayed at home while still being seduced by the plethora of television food shows and the unstoppable flow of cookery magazines and glossy books, might well shudder at the very thought of chewing on boiled pigs' trotters splashed with vinegar, salt and pepper or at the way it was, in the kitchen and at the family dining table, in the long ago. Yet for all the limitations on ingredients, imposed by class and geographical boundaries or by wartime rationing; for all the lack of gadgetry and facilities, we more than got by: we were contented and we were filled, even if for many there was considerable lack of appropriate vitamins and dietary balance. We didn't, for examples, see many bananas or oranges through the war, though allotments and pots and earth patches in even tiny backyards produced vegetables and some fruits.

Towards war's end and then into early peacetime there were special and wonderful treats for us children to seek, like great explorers knowing where to unearth grand treasures. Exclusive to our part of Southend, we had the Clarke's fish and chip shop on the seafront and there were times of day when we could hand over an old penny for a bag of crispy bits and batter bits that were scooped from the great fryers and heaped in a compartment alongside, so that a fraction of the oil and grease might drain away. A bagful of such leftovers was fabulously finger-licking good long before such a slogan floated across the Atlantic.

And then, in Chase Road, across the rail bridge from Southchurch Hall School, there was the Price's bakery. In late afternoon, when most customers had long since bought their bread and cakes and when we were about to head for home after our lessons, we could buy for a penny or two a bag of leftovers – the crumbs and currants, pastry flakes, coconut strips and colourful decorations and pieces of icing that had fallen from the displays of goodies and into wooden trays beneath. To reach one's sticky fingers into a scoopful of this magnificent mix, in a paper bag, was to reach for heaven.

18

AND so that, then, was that: a childhood as simple, yet as wonderful, as a bag of cake crumbs and the sweepings of the confectionery collection; a childhood that seemed, in retrospect, to disappear almost as quickly as the contents of one of those marvellous paper bags from the bakery which itself also disappeared in the massive changes in my lifetime, the independent and the small giving way to the combined and the mighty.

Now, at such distance of time, when those first, few formative years are beyond a horizon in the deepest reaches of the mind, the contrast between then and today, between that period from mid-thirties to late forties and this dawn of a new millennium, seems more far-fetched than far away. Could our lives have been so innocent and so lacking, in so many ways, compared with the childhood years of later generations and today's?

In a word, in response to every question to or from a survivor of World War Two and from each side of it, the answer is – Yes. We had very little, materially, yet we had so much. We were ignorant about a world that had not reached us through television and satellites and faster-than-sound planes and telephones and then the fax machines and then the internet. We were clerks, not computer operators. We were more disciplined – or even docile, perhaps – and far less revolting.

In our own autumn we can reflect that in our long-ago springtime, nothing much except the seasons changed dramatically. The days and the weeks and the years slipped by in a pattern and a routine largely undisturbed. Families, friends, neighbours mostly were constants so we knew who we were, where we were and we knew almost everyone and everything within our immediate compass. Then the war came and with it we began to experience the changes that would gather in pace and range. Yet even then; even through that first decade that followed the declaration of peace, what became known as progress did not necessarily leave us behind. Not in the manner and in the speed that would mark the sixties and every year since then.

We were not so inquisitive or acquisitive a society, back then. We did not pry through the all-seeing, all-intrusive camera eye into other people's lives and homes and countries. We were not influenced by persuasive and persistent and insistent commercialism. We were often hard up, looking for the next pay day or opportunity to earn or make a few bob, yet we did not worship money. We skimped and saved and went without, that we might then eventually have enough to afford some supposed luxury.

We were far less demanding, nowhere near as challenging, more easily satisfied, more law-abiding and obedient. So, in younger eyes, we might well be seen as boring and even silly.

Who would opt to return to coal fires rather than central heating, tin tub bathnights rather than twice-a-day showers, a walk to work rather than driving one's own comfortable, so-sophisticated car? Who would surrender world-ranging television and computer linkups for an old-fashioned wireless set and Radio Luxembourg or the American Forces Network or the Dutch-language Radio Hilversum as the only alternatives to the Home, Light or Third programmes from the BBC?

Who would abolish the telephone and bring back the telegram boy? Who would abandon wining and dining at the smartest of restaurants in favour of Sunday roast lunch, at home, with all the family at the table? Who would really seek to go back to the corner shop to wait to be served the groceries from the shelves and cupboards and beneath the counter, from Mondays to Saturdays, with half-day closing Wednesdays and never on Sundays, rather than wander the rich and packed aisles of vast supermarket, choosing for themselves and checking the quality and quantity for themselves?

Who would opt for a fortnight at Southend's seaside instead of a Caribbean cruise?

Would you turn back the clock, if there then could be no return to the present? Only those who truly recall the distant yesteryear might be able to answer such a hypothetical question, and then only with reservations. Of course it would be wonderfully wonderful to be able to live life again, to get a second chance to appreciate and cherish and make the most of every single day. But there would be considerable prices to pay for going back in time, just as the cost of moving forward has been high.

Every step ahead has meant stepping on someone or something, in the way that despised ruthless businesses and business leaders are said to move ahead and upwards. Increased affluence has meant a high price to traders in Southend and to the town itself: more and more people shop elsewhere and travel farther afield for leisure and pleasure and holidays. So our town has declined as a seaside resort and as a shopping centre. This is clear to witness in the decay and despair that affects so many parts of the whole.

The car that was once an impossible dream for so many of us, long since became stark reality and brought with it a nightmare of its own. It choked our roads and streets, bred violence of thought and deed among even the previously sane and sedate and spawned and fed the relentless crimewave. Before the car we walked; and we usually walked in safety.

The journey through life of those now of retirement years has been truly astounding, even frightening. The road has been high and low, smooth and bumpy, sometimes narrow in outlook, sometimes opening to breathtaking views and possibilities. There have been warnings, danger signs, delays, diversions. All the while, the pace and the speed have increased. There may be a dead end somewhere ahead, but that will be a matter for those who follow today's oldies.

For us, there is no going back, other than in the mind. While I for one try mostly to look ahead, I confess to finding considerable pleasure in the occasional journey in the past.